I hope you enjoy

DON'T BELIEVE EVERYTHING YOU THINK!

DON'T BELIEVE EVERYTHING YOU THINK!

A Guide to Career Revitalization for Financial Advisors

Steve Luckenbach with Tim Vandehey

Copyright 2010 Steve Luckenbach with Tim Vandehey

ISBN 978-0-557-53888-1

LEAP
Press

CONTENTS

Praise for *Don't Believe Everything You Think:*

"When I think of Steve Luckenbach, I think passion. Steve is passionate about speaking, service and the financial services industry. It gives me great pleasure to recognize Steve for his latest demonstration of passion, his book, Don't Believe Everything You Think*! I know this book will make a significant difference in your life and work."*

—Lou Cassara, CLU, ChFC, President & CEO, The Cassara Clinic & The Financial Resource Network

"Steve Luckenbach is more passionate and alive than anyone I have met. His book should come with a warning: 'This message will be hazardous to the ordinary life.' It is a must read for anyone who wants more out of life."

—Dr. Kevin Elko, Corporate and NFL Consultant and author of The Pep Talk

"As a consultant in my previous life, and as senior executive with our firm, I have hired and watched hundreds, perhaps even thousands of speakers, coaches, and consultants. There are those who rely on sheer enthusiasm, and those with a more cerebral approach. Steve Luckenbach is one of the rare talents capable of effectively applying both. His presentations are thoughtful and thought provoking, instructional and enlightening, and passionate and motivating. He pulls no punches in shining the light on both successes and failures—not only for the industry, but himself as well. He is a guy who walks the talk and has achieved the success he wants others to share. For those who can't get to one of Steve's presentations, this book serves as the next best thing."

—Greg Salsbury, Ph.D., Executive Vice President, JNLD, Author of Retirementology: Rethinking the American Dream in a New Economy

"It starts like a joke—'A stockbroker, banker and financial planner walk into a bar...'—but ends with much, much more. I'm not typically a huge fan of business parables, but this is an important exception. The depth of Steve's ideas and the character interplay are unusual for the genre. Steve has created a book that will not only transform the work of financial professionals, but can help change the life of anyone."

—Roger Hall, Ph.D., Business Psychologist, Compass Consultation, Ltd.

Preface

I've been a wholesaler of financial products for more than 20 years, and during that time I've done plenty of speaking to financial advisors, but it was only four years ago that I started speaking professionally. What happened? Well, a few years ago I crossed a personal Rubicon—reached a point of no return and stepped over it, never to look back. I realized that my life wasn't working out the way that I thought it would and that the things I thought were truly important really weren't. I'll go into more detail about that later on, but for now let's just say that I found myself at a place where I either had to reinvent myself and my career or lose everything. There was too much good to give up, so I chose to change things. Radically change things.

Part of that change was that I started to develop a lot of original thoughts. I realized that in the first 15 years of our careers most of us are just repackaging other people's ideas. We're doing what we think we're supposed to do, because that's what everyone else is doing. Coming from a place where I had to reexamine *everything* about who I was and what I was working for as a financial professional, I found myself flooded with ideas and concepts. The more I started sharing those concepts in workshops with advisors, the faster the audience members started writing. They said to me, "I love your material but I couldn't write fast enough. Where can I get your stuff?"

As my company, Jackson National Life Distributors LLC, encouraged me to speak more as part of our outreach efforts, I heard this request many times. There was a grassroots groundswell of encouragement to go beyond the speech and do something that would further impact lives. That positive feedback helped the new ideas come even faster, until I had enough material that I could have spoken for three or four hours. Because a typical speech is only one hour, I knew that ultimately I would have to write a book to say everything I wanted to say without a time limit, to give my audiences what they were asking for, and to have a real chance to have a positive influence on financial advisors—and through them, their clients.

The funny thing was that I was attracting this intense interest while saying things that were anything but comfortable or reassuring for my audiences to hear. I was sharing with them (and I still do) that most of them were in the business for the wrong reasons: to sell and not to serve. I was asking them to take a brutally honest look at the value they were providing their clients and if they felt truly fulfilled with their careers. Most importantly, I was insisting that the quality most vital to their future success was not their skill as a stock picker or their brilliance at asset allocation but their *humility*.

Humility, I discovered on my own journey, is the path to authentic service. Serving is less of a job and more of a responsibility. To those who have been blessed with humility, their calling, I believe, is to serve those who think they have it all figured out. Inevitably, that leads to arrogance and hubris, overreaching and disaster. Gandhi said that it takes great humility to see the truth; I spent four years conveying to financial superstars that their degrees and certifications mattered little, likely weren't making them happy, probably weren't making their clients lives better, and in the end, were pretty meaningless. They loved it. Clearly I was striking a nerve. A book was inevitable.

The heart of this book is the incredible set of insights I gained about the functioning of the human brain and psychology—specifically, how our brains are naturally wired to make poor financial decisions based on short-term thinking, self-delusion and panic. In my studies over several years, I found an inescapable truth:

The human brain is linear—the markets are not!

Investors keep behaving as though the markets are linear, telling themselves that whatever happened recently will continue. If we're at the top of the market, investors often think it's going to go up forever. If we're at the bottom, they often think it's going to go down forever. They make decisions based on those unconscious conclusions, which is primarily why they buy when shares are at their highest prices and pull their money out after the market takes a dive and prices are at their lowest.

Unfortunately, the behavior of most advisors is no different from the investors they purport to serve! You may be no different from your clients sitting across the desk from you! I wrote this book to assist in opening the eyes of financial advisors who believe that they are only as good as their products—who believe that the only value they provide to customers lies in getting them into products that will often produce those short-term gains that are so satisfying to the brain's emotional centers. *That is not where your true value lies.* This journey is about facing the uncomfortable truth that it is difficult to make serving decisions while relying on the same thought processes and sources of information that your clients rely on. If you read, hear, and see what your clients are reading, hearing, and seeing, you will think how they think. You'll do exactly what they want you to, and that is often not in their or your best interest.

The greatest financial advisors serve their clients by giving clients what they *need*, not just what they want. What clients often want is to give in to panic and fear; what they need, however, is for you to lead them—focusing not on the latest, greatest product and short-term gains or losses but on a long-term picture that includes their values, passions, and goals. The sheep don't need a sheep; they need a shepherd.

Sounds good, right? Here's the kicker: you likely won't serve your clients in that way while you are convinced that your value lies in your products and your ability to pick investments. When you base your worth as a professional on the market, I submit that you're only as good as the market. You will always run back to product out of the fear that, deep down, product is the only thing of value you have to offer.

My goal with this book is to show you how your brain can sabotage you and inspire you to challenge the purpose of your work. I want to set financial advisors free and change the idea that you are only as good as what they sell. I want your clients to love and value you, and I want you to love and value yourself. I want to make you uncomfortable with stories that upset your preconceptions and sound disturbingly familiar. I want to make you uneasy by asking some difficult questions:

> *What are the choices I have been making?*
> *Why have I been making them?*
> *What lies are those choices based on?*
> *With new truths, can I make different choices?*

Do you need to read this book? Here's the irony: the advisors who need it the most are likely the ones who think they need it the least. They think they've got it all figured out. They have built a client base that matches their capability and comfort level. They've convinced themselves that focusing on short-term gain, shilling products and working endless hours with little to no real purpose is where it's at. It's not. If you're tempted right now to say with a smirk, "I don't need this book," ask yourself this question and answer honestly:

> *"Do I always counsel my clients to do what's best for them or what's easiest for me?"*

If you can honestly say you're about what's best for your clients, even when they fight you on it, bravo. You are one of God's chosen. If you're like the majority of advisors, most of the time you're about selling product and making your numbers. The financial advisor who needs this book is self-aware enough to know that's the way she or he often does business and that it's often empty and unsustainable. The best advisors are always seeking to improve. They take pride in what they don't know, because it means they remain open to learn.

This book is about taking yourself beyond your capabilities and cutting loose clients who aren't ready for the advisor you become. It's about helping your clients grow as you grow. Great advisors are open-minded. They recognize that the transforming truths in life lie in its paradoxes. When everyone is buying, sell. When everyone is selling, buy. It is better to give than receive. Love your enemies. Run toward danger. Relish your fear. These statements force you to think outside the box.

Our journey is made up of seven lessons, each of which leads to the next:

1. Understand your brain and how its natural wiring provokes erroneous thinking and bad decisions despite what you think you know.
2. Know the importance of facing the brutal truth.
3. Discover why you do what you do.
4. Learn why doing what's right is everything.
5. Motivation is not enough—you need inspiration.
6. Put yourself in position to have an epiphany about your career and life.
7. Discover the humility to admit that you can't overcome your brain's hard wiring and create systems to ensure that your greater purpose is always served.

This book takes an unusual approach to unusual material: it offers a parable in the form of a Financial Advisor, a Stockbroker, and a Banker who search an abandoned Wall Street to find an ancient guru of great wisdom. The guru dispenses lessons that are funny, perplexing, poignant, and always effective, together with plenty of stories and quotes from brilliant authors like Jim Collins and Lou Cassara. There's something in *Don't Believe Everything You Think* for everyone, including some extra goodies I've thrown in at the end for flavor:

- Luckenbach Laws—Dozens of important statements related to this material, worth memorizing and suitable for framing.
- Luckenbach Lines—Great epigrams containing timeless wisdom from some of the most amazing

minds in science, medicine, business, finance, politics, religion and literature.

- Luckenbach Leaps—Bits of quick advice designed to help you take important steps on the road to self-transformation.

In the end, this book is much more than a distillation of my speeches or a treatise on the brain and finance. It's a model for the future of your profession, perfect for anyone who's tired of careening from exhilaration to depression based on the ups and downs of markets and economies. There is limitless freedom in letting go of assets and products as metrics of how much you are worth and how much value you create. This book will help you reinvent your career. It will give you the tools to help your clients reinvent their lives and free them from damaging cycles.

We are all limited by the simple fact of being human. We didn't choose to wire our own brains, but we can choose which values define us, and we can choose to act from a place of purpose rather than profit, knowing that if we do, profit will take care of itself. When all is said and done, we are in control. Are you ready to unlearn everything you know about being a financial advisor? I promise it will be quite a ride.

Steve Luckenbach

July 2010

Introduction

A Financial Advisor, a Stockbroker, and a Banker Walk into a Bar . . .

There was not a car on Wall Street. No hurried men and women in power suits crowded the sidewalks, each in a bigger rush than everyone else. The sidewalks were as empty as the streets. It was like a ghost town, maybe as quiet as it had been before the days when the Dutch arrived in the 17th century and there was an actual timber and earth wall that marked the boundary of the settlement known as New Amsterdam. The only sound was the song of birds, something that usually went unnoticed at 9:30 on a Wednesday morning.

The Financial Advisor, his suit unwrinkled but his brow deeply furrowed, picked his way carefully along the sidewalk. He carried an expensive briefcase, wore a gold watch and expensive Italian leather shoes; he was the very picture of the successful middle-aged financial professional. But he looked disoriented, even frightened by the tomblike silence of this normally frantic, bustling part of Manhattan. Where was everyone? What could have possibly happened to clear every living soul out of the busiest financial district in the world?

"Hello? Is anybody there?" No answer. He crossed Pearl Street toward what had once been a bustling financial building and was now a seemingly empty skyscraper. No one was in sight; not a single taxicab plied the canyons between the tall buildings. The Financial Advisor couldn't figure it out: what kind of disaster could have occurred? Could it have been another terrorist attack? A plague? A crime wave? Global warming? He couldn't think of anything that could bring New York's entire economic machine to a standstill. Still he walked on past two curious pigeons, the clicking of his heels loud in the echoing silence.

The Stockbroker

"You there!"

When the voice broke the stillness, the Financial Planner nearly jumped out of his expensive shoes. He looked around frantically. "Hello?" he said. He saw a woman in a well-tailored gray pinstripe suit walking slowly down the steps of another building that now stood as a monument to the dangers of hubris and capitalism.

The Stockbroker approached the Financial Advisor as if she had seen a ghost. Her eyes were sharp and intelligent, but she wore the same shell-shocked look he was sure was on his face. He could see that she was tempted to reach out and poke him with a finger to see if he was real and not just an illusion brought on by too many hours in front of a Bloomberg box and too much coffee. Instead, she said, "Do you know what's going on?"

"Nobody's in your office, either?" he said. His hope for answers was deflating like a child's party balloon.

"Not a soul. It's usually wall-to-wall brokers and deals in there, but you could hear a pin drop this morning. I know, because I actually dropped a pin to see, and . . ."

"You could hear it?"

"Clear as a bell." This was getting stranger. For her part, the Stockbroker looked more irritated than worried as she checked her watch and looked at her Blackberry for the tenth time in the last ten minutes. She hadn't gotten her Series 7 license just to play Twenty Questions with a stranger while there was money to be made! For his part, the Financial Advisor was just relieved that he wasn't losing his mind.

"Well, I don't know what's happening, but I'm going to keep looking for other people," he finally said. "Someone's got to have some answers. Would you like to join me?"

She looked at her watch again, shoved the Blackberry in her purse, shrugged and said, "Why not? There's not much else I can do in this ghost town, is there?" They fell into a similar stride as they continued walking north, up the island, both looking left and right for any signs of life.

The Banker

An hour went by and they continued to walk. It grew warmer; the Financial Advisor took off his coat and rolled up his sleeves. Subway trains rumbled beneath their feet on their way north toward Midtown, and they both wondered if there was anyone on them. They were within sight of the East River when they crossed into a paved courtyard and found a man of about 30 years old with his coat off, his necktie knotted around his forehead like a biker's headband, his briefcase fallen open, and his papers scattering to the winds. He stared blankly ahead as they walked up to him, both excited that finally they might get some news.

The Banker was not having a good morning. He'd run out of gas on the Long Island Expressway. He had been late for an important meeting with bank regulators. And finally, when he had arrived at that meeting, no one else was there. The entire office was empty. He waited in the conference room for an hour (he'd entertained himself by eating all the donuts in the refrigerator, including the jellies, which were usually claimed by the executives), and then waited at his desk for another hour. Now he was waiting for . . . something. Possibly a massive case of indigestion? He didn't know.

The Stockbroker wasted no time in grilling him. "Who have you seen? What do you know?" she barked.

The Financial Advisor was a little more cautious. "Do you have any idea what's happened to everyone?" he asked gently.

The Banker stared straight ahead, then in a deep and pleasant voice said, "No one. Nothing. No. How's that?" His brow furrowed. "Maybe we're the only survivors of some massive epidemic, like in that Stephen King novel. Perhaps we've been chosen to repopulate the earth." Both men turned to look at the Stockbroker, who folded her arms.

"Not a chance, gentlemen. That's not even on my calendar until 2013." She showed them her Blackberry calendar. The calendar function for August 28, 2013 clearly read, "Childbirth 10 a.m. Pedicure 4 p.m." Wordlessly, the Financial Advisor held a hand out to the Banker and pulled him to his feet. Both men headed down the street toward the river, the Stockbroker trailing, arms out, asking, "What?"

The trio wandered in and out of financial buildings, headquarters of economic titans, finding nothing, and hearing nothing but the humming of air conditioning units. They came upon electronic displays that should have shown the numbers from the markets but now were blank LCD panels.

The Guru

Finally, nearing the edge of the Financial District, they passed a dim, narrow side street, and all three distinctly heard the unmistakable clang and ring of a pinball machine. It echoed down the tight walls of what was almost an alley between the tall buildings. The three looked at each other in astonishment, then as one, ran into the dark lane toward the sound, their heels clicking on the stained concrete and old brick. As they got closer, they realized that the sound was coming from a low building decorated with neon signs for various light beers. A bar, albeit one with no name that anyone could see. The racket of dinging bells was clearly issuing from inside the cinderblock walls.

The Financial Advisor, Stockbroker, and Banker gave each other dubious glances. To stay outside and wander the streets was intolerable. To duck into a dark bar and who knows what kind of situation with an unknown pinball wizard seemed preferable to what they had been doing all morning. The Financial Advisor stepped forward, opened the wooden door, held it for the Stockbroker, and then followed her in. Still slightly dazed, the Banker almost walked into the closed door, then yanked it open and strode into the dim tavern.

The scene was every urban back-street bar cliché come to life: a long, low bar backed with bottles and bottles of cheap liquor, sawdust and peanut shells on the floor, a jukebox, tall tables with barstools, and side-by-side dartboards awaiting a game. What wasn't standard issue was the gentleman hunched over the pinball machine in the corner, hips swiveling, head jerking back, and legs pistoning as he tried to will the chrome ball to go where he wanted it to go.

He looked like the love child of a psychedelic band member and an actor from a 1960s TV show: a tidy gray beard, lean body clad in jeans, biker boots, a fatigue jacket over a tie-dyed t-shirt, and a New York Yankees baseball cap. He shimmied and twisted over his game, ignoring the trio that had just entered his space. They walked over and stood behind him, utterly nonplussed by the entire situation. The flashy graphics of an Elton John album from the 1970s grinned back at them from the game. What now?

"Blast!" The Guru (for that's who he was) slammed his flat palm on the glass of the machine as his last ball disappeared down the hole. He stood, removed his hat, and wiped sweat from his shiny bald head. "Seventy-eight thousand. Not bad. Not bad." He was taller than he had seemed at first, and he turned and faced the three footsore and overheated professionals. "Well?"

"Well what?" answered the Financial Advisor.

The Guru grinned, showing rows of perfect white teeth. He could have been 40, or 70, or somewhere in between. "Well, you'd like to know what's going on here on Wall Street today, wouldn't you? Why it's a ghost town? That does interest you three, doesn't it?"

The Stockbroker stepped forward, tottering on her high heels. "You know what's happened to everyone in New York?"

The Guru smiled again, walking over to and then behind the bar, where he started grabbing glasses. Seemingly without will, the three followed him and each took a place on a stool. They could see their reflections—sunburned, disheveled and a little stunned—in the mirrored wall behind the bottles. The Banker started munching martini olives; the Stockbroker grabbed a compact out of her purse and worked on her makeup.

The strange man dropped his first bombshell. "It's not everyone in New York. It's just the Financial District. If you'd gone a few blocks north or south to Battery Park, you would have seen plenty of people going about their business on a typical work day. Why do you assume the world revolves around you and your pursuit of more?" He hefted a silver shaker. "Drink?"

The three stared at each other. They had assumed that the streets were deserted throughout Manhattan, perhaps the entire city of New York, maybe the entire country! It hadn't occurred to them that it could just be Wall Street. "How do you know that?" the Banker said around a mouthful of garish red Maraschino cherries.

"Been looking around. Watching. Central Park, Broadway, the Meatpacking District, all busy as ever. It's only here that everyone decided to stay home for the day, assuming someone else would cover for them." The Guru poured a drink and slammed it home with relish. "Ah, that hits the spot. You ever ask yourself what would happen if everybody decided to take the day off all at once?"

"That's what's happened?" said the Financial Advisor.

"Best as I can tell. I think everyone in your lines of work came down with the same sickness all at once and decided that they just couldn't get themselves to come to work. It's a pretty common disease, you know, especially today in America."

"What disease? Is it contagious?"

"Hardening of the passion. Progressive atrophy of the ability to find meaning in the numbers and transactions. Call it what you like. And yes, it is very contagious. In fact, you three already have it. Are you sure you won't have a Harlem Stinger? It's one hell of a belt." The Guru held out a highball glass brimming with a noxious-looking brown liquid.

"Not for me," said the Financial Advisor. "It's still a work day." The Stockbroker and Banker also demurred. The Banker's mouth was now stuffed with pearl onions.

The Guru pulled up a barstool of his own and sat down, then poured three tall glasses of sparkling soda water and added wedges of lime. "Models of moral rectitude," he said with a slight smile. "Impressive. Here, you must be thirsty after all that walking." They each took a soda water and sipped. "I'm not talking about some kind of anti-finance mindset, by the way," the man said. "There's nothing wrong with wealth creation, pursuing money or any of that. It's just that I think many of the people in the financial world have become rather . . . lost."

The Problem

"Lost," the Stockbroker said, mouthing the word like a sip of bad wine. "You mean the entire financial industry is suffering some sort of moral malaise and people decided to stay home from work all at once because they couldn't think of a reason to go?"

The Guru smiled. "You're quick. That's exactly right. Your profession has lost its way. Most people aren't working to serve others anymore; they're working to sell product and take home a paycheck. Over the long term, nobody can sustain that sort of existence. Eventually, you burn out or give up and become a robot, going into the office every day on autopilot because you can't think of anything better to do or you're too afraid to change. Eventually, your clients get hurt, because instead of thinking creatively and originally and handling their finances with a purpose in mind, you're thinking exactly like they are, with fear, ignorance, or greed."

Silence. The trio didn't look at one another but stared down at their drinks. "Hit a little close to home, I'd say," said the Guru softly, sipping his own beverage. They could all hear the 1950s-era clock ticking away behind the bar. "Hit close to home for the majority of folks who do what you three do. Most have gotten away from serving something greater than themselves and become product pushers and sales machines. That's no way to lead a fulfilling life, and it's certainly no way to keep an economy from slipping into a cycle of boom-bust, boom-bust, which is what we have now."

"So what are you suggesting?" said the Financial Advisor. His eyes were focused, hard and sharp, on the bearded man. "Get out of the business? Give up what we know? Start over?"

"No! Of course not! You don't throw the baby out with the bathwater!" the Guru said with a scowl. "Like I said, there's nothing inherently wrong with pursuing wealth or helping people to grow their worth. It's just that . . ." He trailed off, seemingly lost in thought, stroking his long beard with his left hand while his right poured a gin and tonic seemingly on its own.

"That what?" The Banker had spoken the least of the three but now he was fired up, perhaps because he had consumed everything edible at the bar. His eyes burned with curiosity. "It's just that what? Don't leave us hanging, man."

The Guru fixed his gaze on the young man. "Most folks seem to have forgotten why they are pursuing or helping to grow wealth," he said slowly and clearly. "Friedrich Nietzsche said, 'He who has a *why* to live can bear almost any *how*.' Why are you in business? Why do your clients need you? Why do you help others build wealth? What is your purpose? Do you define your worth by your net worth? Those are the questions no one is asking, and they are the questions everyone is asking."

The Banker stared, transfixed. The Financial Advisor looked down, seemingly embarrassed. The Stockbroker was having none of it. "I don't have time for this," she barked. "I have to get back to my office." She rose, turning and preparing to leave.

"And do what?" the Guru snapped. "Sit in your office staring at your computer and waiting for five o'clock? Get up tomorrow and forget all this happened, then spend the next 30 years doing the same thing you do now, working 70-hour weeks, living for the weekend and promising yourself that tomorrow you'll get out of your rut and do something meaningful?"

The Stockbroker stopped dead in her tracks and whirled on her heel, prepared to lash out at the Guru.

"You *already* do something meaningful!"

She stopped dead, her mouth open.

"You help people realize their dreams! But you and the majority in your profession don't know it or do it for the right reasons. Most of you have all the technical, financial, and sales skills in the world. That's not your problem. What you lack is the why! That's why Wall Street is empty today: almost everyone who works in it is empty. Rudderless, bereft of purpose or meaning. Richard Leider said, 'The purpose of life is to live a life of purpose.' What's your purpose, ma'am?"

The Stockbroker slowly walked back to the bar and sat down on her stool.

"What's your purpose, mister banker?" he continued. "What's yours, financial advisor?"

More silence. Titans of the financial world only hours before, the trio looked at the pitted wooden surface of the bar like schoolchildren who had been rebuked by a teacher.

"Well, that was quite a speech," said the Guru. He stirred his drink, took a test sip, and let out a satisfied sigh. "I do go on when I get revved up. But I think you see my point."

"Which is?" said the Financial Advisor, wiping sweat from his brow, despite the coolness of the dark bar.

"There's nothing wrong with what you do," the Guru said. "What's wrong is how you do it and why you do it. You and your entire profession are infected with what you could call cancer of purpose. Late stage. Very nasty."

"Is there a cure?" asked the Financial Advisor.

The Lesson

The Guru grinned, drained his glass, and stood tall, stretching and touching the low ceiling. "That, my friend, is the question. Yes, there is a cure. It's called becoming awake, aware of truth. Enlightened, you might say. Any of you go to church?"

The Stockbroker shook her head. She had been raised Catholic but lapsed long ago. The Financial Advisor shrugged.

The Banker smiled. "Eight days of Hebrew school," he said. "They kicked me out for asking too many questions."

"Rebel. Good for you," the Guru said. Well, to be inspired, some say, is to be in spirit, and if you can't find it in church, it's best you look elsewhere. For many, religion has become a path to avoid Hell, but the irony is that spirituality most often comes to those who have already been through Hell.

Living a purposeless life could be defined as a living Hell. But adversity can be a blessing if we learn from it. Fire can burn out the impurities and the lies we live by and set us free on the other side. That's a freedom that comes from knowing the truth.

"What the hell do you want from us?" The Stockbroker frowned as her hands gripped the bar.

The Guru placed one of his hands over hers, and though the others expected her to recoil, she did not. The man's hands were warm and callused like a sailor's and were free of jewelry. Slowly, her hand closed around his and held it. "I think you three were sent here to take this message to the rest of your profession," he said quietly. "I think that's why you're the only ones on the street and why you found your way to this dive—which, by the way, has a wicked blues jam every Sunday."

"What do you want us to do?" the Financial Advisor said.

"Stay. Listen. Learn. Understand," the Guru replied. "Let me be your guide and teach you what I mean when I say that your profession needs to find the why before you can really serve the people you are trying to serve—and serve yourselves as well."

The Banker grinned. "Dude, shouldn't you be on top of a mountain somewhere, wearing sackcloth or something?"

"Maybe, but then you wouldn't have found me. I think this place works much better as a mountaintop: closer, more comfortable, and there's beer and music. Plus, ma'am, you'd have one hell of a time climbing the Himalayas in your five-hundred-dollar shoes."

Still holding the man's hand, the Stockbroker cracked her first smile since the trio had met. Simultaneously, the three of them realized that the Cold War-era neon clock behind the bar was broken, its hands stuck at 2:35. It was as if they were in a timeless space, dark and calm, where they could absorb whatever this strange man wanted to share with them. If they opened the door back into the daylight and the alley, would the spell be broken?

"So what do you say? Are you ready to stay and listen?" the Guru asked.

"I'm in," said the Financial Advisor.

"Let's do it, bro," said the Banker.

"I'm not going anywhere," said the Stockbroker.

The Guru clapped his hands, making a sound like a gunshot, a shocking sound in the quiet bar. "That's the spirit! Okay, first things first, I need—" He spun on his heel until his gaze fell on the chalkboard that a bartender presumably used to list the night's special drinks. "Yes! Let me write a few things down before we get started." He grabbed a piece of chalk and began to write in a large, clear script while the others watched.

Blame it on your brain
Brutal truth
What do you serve?
Do what's right
Knowledge isn't enough
Put yourself in a position to have an epiphany
Be humble

"What's all that?" said the Banker.

"Those, my young apprentice, are the lessons I'm going to share with you," the Guru said, his voice gaining depth and richness. "I'm going to ask you some horribly hard questions and demand answers. I'm going to make you peer into yourselves, especially the parts you don't want to see. I'm going to destroy your self-delusions. You're probably going to weep and hate my guts before this is done. Doesn't that sound great?"

"Sounds like hell," said the Financial Advisor.

"Right. What did I say about truth and spirituality? And what do you have to do if you want to get incredibly fit or become a black belt in karate? You have to work, sweat, and get your butt kicked by a trainer or a sensei. Welcome to class, children, only there's no need to bow. But I promise that this will change everything about what you do. Are you ready?"

The trio looked at each other. This was clearly a Rubicon moment. They could all get up, drain their tonic water, and parade out into the dying afternoon light and New York noise to whatever normal life would bring them. As they met each other's eyes, they all knew that was the last thing anyone was going to do. They swiveled on their stools back to the bar in unison, like a drill team.

The Financial Advisor, who seemed to have become the spokesman, said it for them all. "We're in."

"Outstanding!" The Guru said, rubbing his hands together. "Before we get going, son?" He addressed the banker. "Would you go over to the jukebox and play us a tune? I could really use some atmosphere. You don't need to put in any money; I know the management."

The Banker shrugged, got up, shuffled over to the brightly lit machine, searched its buttons and selections, and after a few seconds pressed a button. As he returned to his barstool, the sophisticated syncopation of "Take Five" filled the bar.

The Guru sighed. "Dave Brubeck. Perfect." He quickly made another drink, cracked his knuckles, leaned on the bar, and addressed his new charges. "Settle in, children. I'm going to tell you a story about that little space between your ears, because it's the key to everything."

So it began.

PART I
THIS IS YOUR BRAIN ON HUMANITY

Lesson One

The Four Most Dangerous Words in Investing (And Why Everyone Says Them)

> *"Until you make the unconscious conscious, it will direct your life and you will call it fate."*
> —Carl Jung

> *"Success, like happiness, cannot be pursued; it must ensue, and it only does so as the unintended side-effect of one's dedication to a cause greater than oneself."*
> —Victor Frankl, *Man's Search for Meaning*

> *"What you are speaks so loudly, I can't hear what you say."* —Ralph Waldo Emerson .

> *"Who you are being is far more important then what you are doing."* —Lou Cassara, *From Selling to Serving*

Do any of you know about Dr. Daniel Kahneman?" the Guru asked.

Silence.

"He won the Nobel Prize in Economics in 2002, even though he's not an economist. He's a psychologist who specializes in the psychology of judgment and decision-making, behavioral economics, and hedonic psychology, the psychology of pleasure. He said that he felt overconfidence was the single greatest factor in investor failure. In other words, our confidence in our linear conclusions is what trips us up most often. Dr. Kahneman knows that we're a bundle of biases: expectancy bias, recency bias, confirmation bias—"

"There was a basketball player named Len Bias a few years back," the Banker interrupted.

This earned him a glare from the Guru. "I trust you've all heard of a gent named Albert Einstein?" Nods all around. "Well, Einstein came up with this equation you might also have heard of: $e = mc^2$. His version has to do with the potential amount of energy contained in the nuclear forces at the heart of the atom, but that's not part of what we're talking about. No, for us $e = mc^2$ means this." He erased the chalkboard and wrote:

$$Expectations = Market\ Correction2$$

"Whoa," said the Financial Advisor.

"Exactly," said the Guru. "The more persistent our expectations that the market will continue to move in the direction it has moved based on the past, the more disruptive the results of the inevitable correction. For our discussion, let's say if you take our expected return and square it, that number will represent the losses suffered when the market defies expectations that were never fully supported by reality in the first place."

"Let me put numbers to that example," said the Stockbroker. "If I expect to make 12 percent in a bubble market, then I would lose 144 percent when that bubble bursts? That doesn't make any sense. You can't lose more than 100 percent."

The Guru smiled. "That's correct—if you're thinking about losses only as being directly from your portfolio. But let's use 10 percent instead, which means you would lose 100 percent. As we have seen historically, even the most dire market corrections typically don't cost investors 100 percent of the value of their assets. So how do we account for the remaining amount? How about the loss of a home? The wreckage of a marriage over financial difficulties, which is very common? The loss of health due to stress? Lost income when depression ruins your productivity? The incalculable loss of peace of mind? When you factor all those losses in, I assure you it can easily equal the square of your expectations."

Money and the Brain

The trio was clearly in deep thought about that. None of them had ever factored collateral or personal losses into the equation of market losses; that wasn't professional, was it? They reflected on their own experiences and those of their clients. Financial loss always produced collateral damage: anger, panic, other financial calamity. These losses were predictable in hindsight, so why did people keep making the same mistakes over and over again?

"You're wondering, when the losses were so inevitable and obvious, why people still make bad financial decisions that led to big losses, aren't you?" said the Guru.

The three professionals looked at each other in surprise.

The Financial Advisor spoke up. "I think that's exactly what we were all thinking, but here's my question: why didn't we already know the answer? We're financial professionals. We have degrees, years of training, certifications and experience. Why don't we already know this and take it into account?"

"Because you're human," the Guru said. "Your brain is wired to trip you up. It is designed in such a way that reason, which is what you think drives your decisions, is not always in control. The reason you're dissatisfied is because you're human and your humanity often leads you to make choices out of fear instead of courage. Human fear is the primary risk factor in your business, not the markets. Have any of you ever heard of the amygdala?"

The Banker raised his hand. "Is that one of those weird smart cars they're building in China?"

"No, Einstein, it's a part of your brain," snapped the Stockbroker. She looked to the Guru. "Right?"

"A gold star for the lady," he said kindly. "The amygdala is a part of the brain—actually two parts of the brain, each about the size of an almond, located deep within the temporal lobe. It's the part of the brain that controls what's known as the fight-or-flight response, which was useful when we were trying to escape saber tooth tigers twenty thousand years ago, but less useful now that we're trying to escape boom-bust market cycles. In fact, the amygdala and the behavioral responses we've developed to compensate for its effects are the worst enemies not only of your client's ability to make sound financial decisions but your ability to be the kind of professionals you aspire to be. Shall I go on?"

Nods all around.

"Good. The amygdala is the source of our fear and rage," the Guru continued. "When the amygdala is activated, it shuts off our ability to think rationally. Did you know that, according to a study conducted by Diane Halpern and Stanley Coren and published in *The New England Journal of Medicine* in 1991, left-handed people are five times more likely to die in a car accident than right-handed people, by a rate of 7.9 percent to 1.5 percent? Why would that be?" He paused.

"Let's say you are driving down the road at 60 miles an hour. A car slams on its brakes in front of you, sending an instant visual message through your optic nerve to your brain. Before your frontal cortex—the rational analytical part of your brain—can react, the amygdala sends an explosive message to the adrenal glands sitting on top of your kidneys: YOU'RE GOING TO DIE! The adrenals dump massive amounts of adrenaline into the bloodstream, dilating blood vessels and sending fresh blood into the extremities. At the same time, the amygdala shuts down the immune system and digestive system and suppresses rational thought. The result is an instant fight-or-flight reaction: without thinking, you turn the wheel toward the side of your strongest hand. The left-handed person pulls left. Of course pulling left in this country is problematic. That's where oncoming traffic is. BAM!" He slapped his hand on the bar and they all jumped. "Mourners, please omit flowers," he purred.

"You see, the amygdala's job is to deal with the most immediate threat. It does not consider the long term. That's the job of the neocortex, which gives us our ability to anticipate and plan for the future and predict possible outcomes. Sometimes this can benefit us, but other times? You're walking along the edge of a cliff and slip. As you're falling, you grab onto a branch. You're hanging, but you can pull yourself back up. Unfortunately, next to your hand is a crevice in the cliff wall, and out of this crevice crawls a tarantula, right on to your hand. Your rational mind may know that tarantulas are harmless, but before it can kick in, your amygdala screams, TARANTULA! You jerk your hand away from the spider...and let go of the branch. Oops. Unless you're Wile E. Coyote, it's all over, Jack."

"What does all this have to do with financial services?" the Stockbroker asked.

"I can see you studied your biology but not your psychology," the Guru responded. "Let me continue and it will become clear. The rational part of the brain does not fully develop until age 25, so in our formative years we largely operate with the oldest part of our brains, based on irrational fears that set a pattern of thinking that we take into adulthood. Maturity has been defined as the ability to delay gratification—to stop and think and do what is in our long-term interest instead of short-term sensory satisfaction. If you want to lose weight, you've got to not eat that cheeseburger now to be 20 pounds lighter in six months.

"All thinking flows first through this system, the limbic system, on its way to the rational brain. That's why investors tend to make irrational decisions out of fear and panic, such as pulling their money out of the market at the bottom and locking in their losses. A financial professional's number-one duty should be to help clients engage the more rational portion of their brains and promote healthier behaviors based on forward thinking and reason rather than on this primitive part of the brain. You're handicapped in this, because you're human. It's human nature to think in the short term and react first with fear and panic over a potential loss or the possibility of missing out on a gain."

Sheep and Shepherds

The Guru fell silent as the trio absorbed this stunning information. Could it be true? Were they as handicapped as their clients by their own hard-wired emotional tendencies? They had all seen customers make horrible financial decisions—decisions that, as advisors, they were legally bound to carry out—because they panicked and lost perspective. Those people were just defying their professional advisors' well-reasoned advice—weren't they? It couldn't be that they were just as susceptible to that kind of emotion-fueled self-sabotage. Could it?

"So what are you saying?" asked the Banker, holding out his glass to indicate that he was ready for another tonic water. "That we're just as clueless as our clients?"

The Guru mixed up another drink, his back to the three. "No, I would never say that," he said over his shoulder. "You're worse."

"What?" The Stockbroker stood, her nostrils flaring. "Listen, you second-rate Gandalf with your Deadhead clothes, I bust my butt to help my clients by giving them the best products I can recommend. It's not my fault that they don't always take it!"

The Guru handed the Banker his drink. "Take it easy, young lady. I meant no offense. I only want to open your eyes to the illusion you're laboring under." He pulled himself onto the barstool that stood behind the bar. "You and those in your profession are different from the people you serve. They don't have your specialized knowledge. They don't choose to make foolish financial decisions; they can't help themselves. You can. Sheep don't need other sheep. They need shepherds. Without a shepherd, the sheep can be led to the slaughter. To be a shepherd, you can't think like a sheep. If you allow yourselves to be driven by the same issues that drive your clients, then you're sheep, and that serves nothing and no one."

The Financial Advisor chuckled. "Buddy, can you spare a brain?" He sipped his drink with a wry smile. "This one's not working very well."

"So, you're saying that we're all wired to make bad financial decisions? Even us, with all our training?" said the Banker.

"No, that's not what I'm saying at all."

"I don't understand."

"No, you don't. That's why you're here."

The Banker spit a lime wedge onto the polished wood of the bar. "Now you're going all Obi-Wan Kenobi on us," he muttered.

The Guru grinned broadly. "I prefer to think of myself more as The Dude from *The Big Lebowski*," he said. "I abide."

"Great movie," said the Financial Advisor.

"What are you trying to say, then?" This was the Stockbroker, who was clearly the cut-to-the-chase member of this exclusive club.

"You know—" The Guru said dug through the bottles below the bar in search of something; clinking sounds were heard, "how the brain processes information through its emotion and fear center?" More clinking. "But you don't know anything about what that makes you do or why." More clinking. "You're light years from the 'Aha!' moment that you need to have." Even more clinking. "Aha!"

He popped up with his prize: a bottle of whiskey. "The finest sipping whiskey ever distilled, lady and gents. Anyone care to join me?" No one answered. "Brewed by one of the great geniuses of the distilling business, a man of singular vision and passion." He poured some of the gold-brown liquor into a glass and sipped reverently. "Oh yes."

"You sound as though you knew the distiller personally," said the Financial Advisor.

The Guru's eyes twinkled. "Let's go on." He set down his glass. "What is the key to successful investing?"

The trio looked at each other, each afraid to give the wrong answer. Finally, the silence became oppressive.

"Stop overthinking. It's very simple. It's four words." He erased the chalkboard and wrote:

Buy low. Sell high.

The three laughed. "It's never just that easy," said the Banker.

"No, it's not," said the Guru. "Do you know why? Because our amygdala prevents us from making sound long-term decisions in favor of split-second reactions. The difference between a decision and a reaction is one factor: rational thought. The thing is, true maturity and true self-awareness mean making rational decisions that in the short term might cause us discomfort or appear to cost us money. That's why psychologists say that people don't become adults until about age 25, when they develop the ability to delay gratification. The amygdala has a lot to do with that. In experiments, deactivating it seems to remove barriers to lust and curiosity, so it may be that it's not as strong in younger folks, who have plenty of lust and curiosity to go around. But mainly, the amygdala drives us to defend against fear, and as a kind of side effect, we seek what's pleasurable."[1]

The Four Most Dangerous Words

"I still don't understand," said the Banker.

"You sure you don't want a belt?" said the Guru, holding out the bottle. "It really helps with the cognitive leaps."

"No, thank you."

"Your call. Let me try to explain it this way. According to the National Association of Realtors, what is the primary source of wealth for most Americans?"

"The stock market?" answered the Stockbroker.

"No."

"Residential real estate?" said the Banker.[2]

"Bingo."

The young man winked. "No Tennessee whiskey necessary."

The Guru tipped his glass to the Banker. "But how does that come about? People come to own valuable assets because their mortgage contracts force them to pay a sum of money every month toward paying off their debt. If you don't pay your mortgage, they're going to foreclose on you and kick you out of your house. If people were left to themselves, most would not choose the short-term pain of writing a mortgage check every month, even for the long-term gain of owning a $500,000 house in 30 years. If the system didn't force discipline on them, they would likely blow the money."

"You know," started the Financial Advisor, drumming his fingers on the bar in thought, "401(k) accounts are the same way. People have their contribution taken out of their paychecks automatically, so they are able to save something for retirement. But my clients who are self-employed and have to make the decision to put the money away almost always come up short in their savings goals. They don't have the discipline."

"Exactly!" The Guru slammed his palm down on the bar like a gunshot, making the other three jump. "We are wired to pursue immediate comfort and avoid immediate pain, and only preparation, systems, and discipline can override the amygdala and make us do what is in our long-term interest." He finished his knock of whiskey and set the glass down. "Would you three like to know four of the most dangerous words in investing?"

This got their attention. The Stockbroker, who had been fiddling with her nails, stopped. The Banker sat up straight. "I think we would," said the Financial Advisor.

The Guru erased the chalkboard once again and wrote:

This time, it's different.

There was a long silent pause while they absorbed the words. It was as if a current of energy ran through the simple phrase, and they were plugging into it. They could hear water dripping from the Guru's just-washed highball glass.

The Guru said softly, "They encourage our loss of perspective, terrible decisions and crippling panic. For example, U.S. airlines experience safety issues on about two ten-thousandths of a percent of their flights.[3] Flying is incredibly safe, but if you're in the air and feel some turbulence, all the stats in the world don't matter, because THIS TIME IT'S DIFFERENT. Your amygdala thinks it knows that this plane is going down!"

"I hate flying," said the Stockbroker, looking down at her hands.

The Banker added, "Statistically, it's the safest way to travel."[4]

"He's right, but that doesn't matter. Knowledge is not a defense against the power of the amygdala," said the Guru. "Those drivers who pull left into oncoming traffic know they will die if they pull into the path of an eighteen-wheeler, but they do it anyway. Their amygdala doesn't consider the future, just the immediate need to avoid pain. You can know all the facts and figures on earth, and that won't stop your brain from screaming that your plane is doomed or stop your palms from sweating. You need something else to defend against the design of your brain and to avoid making the same kinds of mistakes that your clients make."

"What is it?" asked the Financial Advisor.

The Guru shook his head. "We'll get to that. You're not ready." He poured himself another glass of whiskey. "Does anyone know what recency bias is?"

"What?" The Stockbroker had stopped playing with her nails and had her eyes fixed on the Guru.

"Recency bias. It convinces us that whatever the most recent pattern has been will continue indefinitely even in the face of overwhelming evidence that it won't. Observe." He reached into his jeans pocket, pulled out a quarter and laid it on the bar. "If I flip this coin, what are the odds it's going to come up heads?"

The Banker piped up. "Fifty-fifty, of course."

"Correct. Now, let's say I flip it 20 times and by some amazing chance, it comes up heads all 20 times. What are the odds of heads the next time I flip it?"

"The same. Fifty-fifty."

"Right again, but recency bias blinds us to this. We start to believe in runs, streaks, magic. It's why we blow on dice or wear lucky scarves in Vegas. Here's something interesting from the research in behavioral finance: losses hurt 225 percent more than gains satisfy.[5] Behavioral scientists interviewed hundreds of people and said, 'Look, a coin toss is fifty-fifty. Heads you lose $100. Tails you win $125. Would you take the bet?' Most people said no, and they said no at $150, $175, and $200! On average, people would not take the bet unless they would win $225 to balance out the potential of losing $100. The wild thing," he continued, "is that recency bias changes the equation. Let's go back to 1999. The market skyrocketed because of the dot-com boom, and even at the top, most people were still investing without any sort of caution. The odds of the coin coming up heads and the market going down hadn't changed, because the odds don't change, but that doesn't matter. When a situation stimulates either our pleasure or fear center, we assume that what has been happening in the recent past is going to continue happening for the foreseeable future. It's a crippling but very human fallacy, boys and girls."

"People say, 'This time, it's different,'" said the Financial Advisor.

The Guru nodded. "Their bias makes them believe that in spite of all the history showing that bubble markets burst and big declines are followed by big rebounds,[6] somehow this time will be different. While there is no way to absolutely know or guarantee what the market will do in the future, throughout the entire history of the market to date, the best time to buy has been when the prices are low—is it really going to be different this time? Yet, even though the market has been consistently cyclical, the majority of people keep doing the same frightened, very human thing that they have been doing and getting positive feedback from others that they are doing the right thing—which gives them the feeling that there is safety in numbers. What trips them up is that the majority is always right—in the moment. That's how it becomes the majority! In the long run, following the herd can ruin you."

The Fear of Death

"You make this sound like a self-esteem thing," said the Stockbroker.

"Savvy leap of logic, ma'am." The Guru was clearly pleased that his students had grasped a point before he stated it. "Everyone wants to be right. In 1997, 1998, and 1999, the guy who put everything in the hottest performing tech fund looked like a genius! The guy who put everything in cash in 2000, 2001, and 2002 looked like a genius. We want to look smarter than the other guy, and that desire—the pleasure of not only making money but looking brilliant—makes us ignore probability in favor of what we want to believe. We get short-term pleasure but most of the time, long-term wreckage."

"The same thing plays out in relationships," said the Stockbroker, and they all turned to look at her. "I was just thinking. I know this woman, a good friend, who has jumped from bad-boy boyfriend to bad-boy boyfriend for 10 years. Every time she meets a new guy, everyone but her can see he's terrible for her. She's obviously thinking, 'This time is different,' and instead, she gets her heart broken again." She sighed. "Is that what you're talking about?"

The Guru nodded. "Go to the head of the class," he said. "Very good. That's not recency bias, but it does point to our ability to delude ourselves based on the idea that somehow, this time is different. We pursue what we *want* when we should be going after what we *need*. Your financial clients know what they want when they come to see you, but it's your job to give them what they need, which is almost never the same thing. That's where most everyone in your profession is falling short. We've done this since we were living in caves, and the circumstances are different but not the behavior. The tools of war are different, but what causes war hasn't changed in 5,000 years. The Bible is 2,000 years old—the writers were on donkeys and we're in Mercedes, but the behavior is the same. The modes of transportation are different but the driver hasn't changed."

"So we're seeing a linear progression where there's a . . . what?" said the Banker. He had removed his tie and coat and rolled up his sleeves, clearly getting into the subject matter.

"A mess. Chaos. Unpredictability. The unknown," said the Guru. "Linear. Human beings are built to grasp at the predictable and linear. We delude ourselves that by finding short-term patterns we can guarantee that those patterns will continue forever. We approach markets in a linear way when the markets are anything *but* linear. Human beings laminate this veneer of false predictability and false continuation onto their world every day, and it leads to boom and bust cycles and massive losses over and over again. Know why we do it?"

Silence.

He smiled slightly. "I think you all know the answer but don't want to say it out loud. It's not something that anyone likes to talk about. Remember when I said that the amygdala is wired to seek immediate comfort and avoid immediate pain? Well, it's also wired to avoid fear, and the greatest fear of every single human being is the fear of the unknown, specifically the unknowable future. Anyone care to venture a guess as to why?"

The Financial Advisor lifted a finger. "Because we all die there."

"Give that man a round of applause." He clapped his hands lightly, breaking the tension in what had become a somber room. "The reason you and your colleagues often lead your clients to make mistakes is because you operate the same way that they do. You make decisions designed to help you avoid the fear of the unknown, because the idea that things will not continue along the linear path that they have always followed reminds us that one day, we won't be here. We don't know when or how we'll die, but we will, so we grant ourselves the comforting illusion of permanence. That's why people have always turned to shamans and seers for predictions—but that's not knowledge. It's speculation."

He put his hands on the bar, leaning forward. "As long as you are making decisions out of fear rather than from courage and service, you will be dissatisfied and forever subject to cycles of boom and bust, gain and loss."

Bias and Ego

"I don't buy it." The Financial Advisor sat bolt upright in his chair, his cheeks reddening. "You're saying we're all puppets of this fear response. My Dad was an Air Force test pilot. They trained the fear response out of him so that he could keep his cool when a plane failed. Navy SEALs, pilots, astronauts, divers—they've all undergone training to overcome the panic response. What about that?"

"That's true," the Guru said. "Conditioning can teach you not to pull left into traffic or to take your money out at the bottom of the market, but most of us can't afford the lesson. If you face the same stimulus over and over again and gradually learn to detach from your fear response, you can overcome it. There's no financial simulator like there is for pilots, so you'll be indigent by the time you figure it out. Plus, you're fighting the single most powerful factor in herd investing: the ego."

"That's true," said the Banker. "Everybody likes to feel smarter than the other guy. That's the whole reason why people share stock tips."

"Yep," said the Guru. "A gentleman named Stuart Wilde wrote this in his book, *Silent Power:* The personality prefers to hear, see, and feel things that please it, or endorse it. The mind focuses on what is congruent with its desires, and eliminates everything else. Perception is thus narrowed by selection.[7] We all have another bias that moves us: confirmation bias. We see only what confirms our already-held beliefs and ignore the rest. In fact, psychologists have found that our brain so completely blocks perception of facts that might create cognitive dissonance so that they truly become invisible to us!"

The Banker snapped his fingers. "Plus, if you don't want to have a belief challenged, you'll avoid information that might contradict it. I know people who are hard-core political conservatives who only watch Fox News and only read conservative Web sites. They won't even look at *The New York Times*. They live in this sequestered world of information that reflects only what they believe."

"Exactly!" said the Guru. "We all do that. It feels good to be right. We know what Jack Nicholson said in the movie *A Few Good Men* when Tom Cruise shouted, 'I want the truth!'"

"You can't HANDLE the truth!" the three yelled in unison.

"And we can't. Back in 2001 and 2002, people who were still hanging in the market after the dot-com crash didn't want to talk about their behavior. Their attitude said, 'Don't talk to me about confirmation bias. I'm in denial right now. That is how I protect my self-esteem. Soon, I'll get to anger, because that's another way I protect it: blaming others.'"

The trio laughed. "Man, have I had some clients like that," said the Stockbroker. "Angry at me and everyone else because of their decisions."

The Guru nodded. "Right. We can't bear to admit that we're not wise and all-knowing. Let's say you own a stock that was up 100 percent last year. To you, this brands you as a smart person. Then the stock plummets because the broad market tanks. Yet we deny. We say, 'It'll come back, it'll come back.' We've become attached. We've become part of a club. Our friends are tech investors. We'd rather follow the path to poverty to stay on the path with our friends. That's the herd mentality, and in the financial world, the herd is almost always slaughtered. It's your job to think like the shepherd and not think like the sheep, your clients!"

The three rocked back on their stools.

He smiled and his face softened. "This really is the core of the message, the core of what you need to know to begin the transformation that your entire industry needs to undergo. Let me ask you all something. What is your primary value proposition as a financial professional? What is it that makes you most valuable to your clients?"

The three students sat quietly, their minds working. None wanted to give the wrong answer, but they didn't know any other answers beyond what had been drilled into them for years.

"Access to financial products," said the Banker.

"Asset allocation," said the Financial Advisor.

"Picking the right stocks and funds," said the Stockbroker.

"Wow," said the Guru. He cracked his knuckles loudly. "Wrong, wrong, and wrong. Your primary value proposition is to help people avoid their own amygdala-driven tendency to panic, make short-term decisions that kill them in the long term, and to let ego, fear, and bias drive their actions. You need to be asking, 'Is this strategy going to work in the real world? Is my client getting real returns that make an impact in their life?' You are selling investment performance when you should be paying attention to investor performance. Your sacred duty is to *not* think like your clients. It is to be disciplined and to give them not what they want but what they need. Here endeth the lesson."

Don't Believe Everything You Think

The Financial Advisor leaned forward. "Wait a second," he said, "you don't think we do that now?"

"I do not," snapped the Guru. "I think you have the knowledge and experience to override your own ego and fear sometimes, but more often than not, you don't. Believe me, you're just as subject to the effects of the amygdala as anyone else. Don't delude yourself into thinking that you don't give financial advice based on what the herd is doing, the desire to be perceived as a genius, and your own fear about the market that ignores the knowledge that all markets are cyclical. Discipline is the way you survive and thrive in cycles, but it's easier not to try to force discipline on clients and just collect a commission for giving them what they want."

The Stockbroker's face was red, perhaps from embarrassment or anger. "It sounds like you're saying we haven't been fulfilling our fiduciary duty," she said through clenched teeth.

The Guru perched his chin on his closed fist. "Legally, technically, you have," he said. "But in the spirit of what you are charged with, which is nothing less than the futures of the people whom you serve, you are not." He unclenched the fist and pointed at her. "They don't and won't have discipline. You must. You must think differently than they do."

"How?" This was the Financial Advisor. He hadn't touched his tonic water, and now downed it all in a gulp. "How do we change how we think?"

"I'm glad you asked," the Guru said. "Have you ever heard the sayings, 'Don't believe everything you read' or 'Don't believe everything you hear'?"

"Of course."

"Well, what I say is 'Don't believe everything you think'. Where do you think your thinking comes from? It's driven by what you watch, listen to, and read. One of the best ways to begin changing how you think and developing the discipline to be a shepherd is to avoid consuming media that enable herd decisions. Avoid the business sections of mainstream newspapers. Stay off the consumer finance Web sites. Purge your mental diet of anything that encourages short-term thinking, panic investing, and overreaction. Read history and observe the behavior. We humans repeat the same patterns again and again, but people who change the world do one thing that most people can't or won't do."

He paused, clearly for dramatic effect, until the Stockbroker finally said, "What?"

"They develop the perspective to see their own patterns and step out of them. They think differently and therefore, they act differently. Knowledge without action is meaningless. If you want to break out of your own patterns, transform yourself, and transform your industry, you must find ways to overcome your brain's hard wiring so that you can do the same for your clients. The first step to doing that is to stop feeding your mind junk food. As a monk once said, 'Stop walking around in my head with your dirty feet.'"

"And that's it?" said the Financial Advisor.

The Guru barked a laugh. "Hardly. I've shared with you the what. You don't know the first thing about the how or why. None of you has the slightest notion of why you're in the business you're in or the most important quality you must possess to do it right. We're just getting started, children."

The three looked around again, gauging each other's reactions. The clock over the bar remained stopped, and it was impossible to gauge the time. No one thought to look at his or her watch or cell phone; it seemed like it might break the spell.

Some silent agreement was reached. The Financial Advisor turned back to the Guru and asked, "So, what's next?"

Lesson Two

The Truth of No Return

> *"All truths are easy to understand once they are discovered; the point is to discover them."*
> —Galileo Galilei

> *"Your time is limited, so don't waste it living someone else's life. Don't be trapped by dogma—living with the results of other people's thinking. Don't let the noise of other's opinions drown out your own inner voice. Most important, have the courage to follow your heart and intuition. They somehow already know what you truly want to become."*
> —Steve Jobs

> *"Risk! Risk anything! Care no more for the opinions of others, for those voices. Do the hardest thing on earth for you. Act for yourself. Face the truth."*
> —Katherine Mansfield

"This is a process, not just a series of lessons."

The Guru was standing near the bar's modern electronic cash register, trying to puzzle out the various colorful touch screens. "What in hell does KOT mean?" he said.

"Kitchen Order Ticket." The Banker spoke from near the jukebox. "I spent seven years as a bartender when I was working my way through school."

"What did you mean about this being a process?" asked the Financial Advisor.

"Well, you're not just here to learn information about how you should be conducting your work," the Guru said. "That's the how. That's just mechanics: what to say to a client and when. That's not going to change things for you, your industry, or the people you serve. No, you're here to discover the why, to find out how you need to change yourselves."

"I kind of thought you'd already told us that," said the Stockbroker. "I was looking forward to getting back to—"

"To the way things used to be?" The Guru wore an ironic, slight smile as he regarded the young woman. "Of course you do. That's what happens when the modern ego encounters the beginnings of truth, especially when that truth threatens to disrupt the comfortable way things are. Sit down and get cozy, and we'll get into this."

It was almost a command, albeit in laconic, grandfatherly phrasing. The Banker ambled back to the bar and flopped on a stool like a college student into a recliner. The Financial Advisor, who had never left his stool, reached over the bar without looking, grabbed a random bottle of liquor, and poured two fingers into his glass. Without looking, he sipped it. "What did I just drink?"

"Anise liquor. You lucked out. It could have been rotgut," the Guru laughed.

The Financial Advisor made a face. "Tastes like licorice."

"That's because it is." He peered at the Stockbroker. "You joining us, ma'am?"

She plopped into a club chair about 10 feet away, clearly put out by her teacher's views on things. "I can hear from over here."

The Guru nodded. "Fine by me. What I meant a moment ago was that if you three walked out of here right now, even with what I've told you about how your brains sabotage everything that you do, you would talk a great game of meaningful change for about a week. Then you would go back to doing everything the same way you did before."

There was a pause before the Stockbroker said, "So what? What's wrong with that? You're acting like there's something wrong with us."

"I never said that." The Guru had retaken his place on his stool; he removed his cap, once again revealing a head so shiny-bald that it looked as though it had never seen a hair follicle. "I didn't have to. You three wandering as aimlessly as you did told me everything I needed to know about you and what you do."

"Okay, enigmatic much?" The Stockbroker spoke in a scornful, angry voice as she stood from her chair. "What is that supposed to mean? Our offices were ghost towns. We were trying to figure out what was going on. What else were we supposed to do?"

The Guru's eyes glowed as he leaned forward, hands clasped. "What indeed," he purred. "Let me ask you this, young lady. Are you happy?"

"What?"

"Are you happy?"

Her eyes took on a defiant cast. "Of course I am," she barked.

The ageless-looking man wasn't buying it. "I didn't ask you if you weren't unhappy," he said. "Do you wake up every day feeling blessed that you get to do what you do? Do you start every week with a sense of anticipation? Do you feel that you're making a positive difference in the world, that what you do matters?"

The woman stared, clearly unsure what to say. The Guru turned his piercing gaze to the two men, who squirmed like students who hadn't done the previous night's assignment and had just been called upon by the teacher. "What about you two?"

The Financial Advisor sighed heavily but said nothing. Seconds ticked by, accreted like minerals from dripping water, and turned into a minute. Finally, the Banker said, "Dude, nobody does that."

"I beg your pardon?" the Guru said.

"Nobody feels that way about what they do." He looked as though the man had just asked him to write out the equations for Fermat's Theorem. "Nobody that I know, anyway. That's some self-help bullsh—sorry, nonsense, that nobody really believes."

"That, young man, is the saddest thing I have ever heard anyone say," the Guru said, "and it's absolutely wrong. There are hundreds of thousands of people who spend their days doing what they are passionately in love with, even in the financial world. Sadly, they are in the minority, but they are out there. Now, I ask you again, are you happy in the way that I described?"

Again, the seconds ticked away. They all looked at the floor as they faced the harsh reality of their individual situation. The weight of the silence grew until finally it became unbearable. "No," whispered the Stockbroker.

"What?" said the Financial Advisor, and he and the Banker swiveled around to look at her.

"I'm not happy," she said, tears starting in her eyes. "I feel like I'm on a treadmill. I get sales goals to meet, and as soon as I meet them, I get new goals that are set a little higher. I meet those, and then I get even higher goals. It's all about more, not better. It never ends. There's no meaning to it. It feels like I spend all my time chasing something that I can't catch and working just hard enough to keep up with all the other mice and not get fired. It's not about the people. It's about survival. I hate it." She caught herself and placed one hand over her mouth, her eyes wide. "I'm sorry."

"Dear, don't be," said the Guru. "This is what we're here for. Do you two gents feel the same way as this brave lady?" He eyed the Financial Advisor and Banker as if daring them to dissemble after their colleague's confession. After a few seconds, they both nodded.

Hacking the Epiphany

"Good. Now we're getting down to honesty. Let me explain what I said about you wandering around aimlessly.

When you showed up for work and found the place utterly abandoned, you didn't know what to do. You felt robbed of meaning. Naturally, you went looking for the thing that gave you meaning: the familiar jobs that you're used to. You were like a tamed horse trained to go back to the barn. The thing is," he continued, "if you truly had meaning in your lives, it wouldn't come from your job. It would come from something inside you and from that which you serve. Someone driven by a deeper meaning to their lives doesn't need an outside resource to serve what gives them meaning; they are driven to find a way to serve, and so they will find it. If your work had genuine meaning for you beyond the money and survival, you would have shown up, found the office empty, said, "Hmm, how weird," and then called your clients and said, 'You know what? I'm coming to your house to go over your account. Is 2:30 okay?' You're all about the how of your business, and that makes you nothing more than a technician. When you know why you do what you do, that will drive the how."

"So what you're saying," said the Financial Advisor, "is that we're kind of addicted to doing things the way we do them—on autopilot, not thinking, mechanically. Right?"

"Exactly right," the Guru said. "Very astute. That's why if you left right now, you'd be back to scrambling to build territory, worrying about making your numbers, shilling products to collect a commission, and dreading Mondays. It may be terrible, but drugs are terrible. Addicts use them anyway. You will go back to the same way you have always worked because it's comfortable and familiar, even though it's miserable. You may know more about why you and your clients make the decisions you make, but that's not enough to—well, let me write this one down."

He erased the chalkboard and wrote:

Knowledge is not sufficient to change behavior.

"Whoa," said the Banker.

The Guru set the chalk down, clearly on a roll now, his voice taking on the cadence of a revival tent preacher. "In the U.S., the self-improvement industry is worth more than $10 billion," he said.[8] "How many of those self-improved people do you think have actually changed their lives in a meaningful way? One percent? Two? That's because knowledge is not enough to motivate you to leave the familiar behind and make disruptive changes. People spend a fortune on books and seminars and feel that because they are acquiring knowledge, they are making meaningful changes. That's self-delusion, and self-delusion is the root of all evil. David Gergen, professor of public service at Harvard's John F. Kennedy School of Government, said it best at the 2009 Willow Creek Leadership Summit: 'Don't confuse motion with progress.'"

He paused for a few seconds to write this pungent phrase on the chalkboard, then continued. "Remember, the amygdala seeks comfort and avoids pain. The familiar is comfortable, even if it makes our rational side miserable. Habit is comforting, but you will not seek meaningful change—disruptive change that takes you out of your comfort zone and scares the living hell out of you—until you can hack the amygdala like a computer thief hacks into a system and give the fearful, passion-driven part of you something more powerful than your fear of change. You won't really discover your why until you have an epiphany."

A few beats passed. They could hear the Stockbroker sniffling a bit, still affected by the emotion of her admission.

Finally, the Banker spoke. "Man," he said, "do you know that you talk like Jerry Garcia?

The Guru laughed. "Yeah, but I can't sing a note," he said.

"An epiphany," said the Financial Advisor. "You mean, a sudden realization of truth?"

"Disruptive truth," said the Guru. "Truth that transforms your understanding in a way that you're not entirely comfortable with, like realizing that the political philosophy you've followed all your life is destructive. Epiphanies reveal what Jim Collins, author of *Good to Great* and *How the Mighty Fall*, calls 'the brutal facts.' I call it something else." He erased the chalkboard and wrote:

The Truth of No Return

"Okay, I'm confused," said the Financial Advisor.

"That's all right," said the Guru. "Certainty is the enemy of change. Confusion is the first step on the road to what the psychologist Abraham Maslow called self-actualization." He sipped his drink. "Truth of No Return is a truth that won't let you go back to the way things were. It's like a one-way security door at the airport: once you've passed through, there's no backtracking. It's like suddenly realizing your spouse is cheating on you; you can't exactly go on and pretend you don't have that knowledge. Truth of No Return is an essential part of an epiphany."

"So," the Banker began, "where can I get an epiphany?"

The Guru started to answer, but a female voice cut him off.

"You can't just order one like it's a pizza." The Stockbroker was walking over to sit on a stool. They noticed that for the first time, she was not holding the handbag she had been clutching like a shield; it sat forlorn on a small cocktail table. "Epiphanies come when they are good and ready, usually when you're anything but prepared for them. That's why they rock your world." She looked at the Guru with shining but dry eyes. "Right?"

"Correct," said the Guru, smiling slightly. "You can't make an epiphany happen, which is why most self-help programs don't work. Yet an epiphany is what we all need in order to change not only how we do things but why we do them. The epiphany overrides the brain's need to cling to the familiar. After you have your epiphany, following your new vision becomes more important to you than fear or discomfort."

"Okay, I'll bite," said the Financial Advisor. "What do you have to do to put yourself in a position to have an epiphany?"

The Truth of No Return

The Guru jumped down from his stool, ran to the other side of the bar and yanked on the rope of the brass last-call bell again and again; shrill metallic peals filled the bar like a cathedral. The three students covered their ears. "The gentleman has just discovered the billion dollar question!" the Guru shouted. "That's exactly the right language, son. No one can make an epiphany come. Most of us don't want one, because it contradicts the way we have been doing things and clashes with our confirmation bias. It demands that we stop doing what we have been doing and do something that might destroy life as we know it."

He strode back to his barstool and sat on it, ramrod-straight. "Most of what we're going to talk about in this bar is going to be about the process of putting yourself in the position to have the epiphany that will transform your career. The first stage in that process is facing your own painful Truth of No Return. Epiphanies reveal that truth to you, but they do it abruptly and sometimes brutally. That's why they turn your life upside down. Doesn't it make more sense to confront your truth yourself, on your own terms?"

They were all nodding. This made sense to people who were used to being in control, prepared for whatever life threw at them—or so they thought.

"Good," the Guru said. "Because—and believe me when I say this—each of you already knows the kind of practice, career, and life that you'd like to have."

This shook them all. They each scanned their mental landscape: Do I really know what I want? Is this true? How could it be true?

The Guru continued. "So what is the truth for each of you? Why do you do what you do, live how you live? Why are you unhappy," he turned to the Stockbroker, "when you know what you really want?" He finished his drink and bent to make another. "Keep in mind that Tertullian said, 'The first reaction to truth is hatred.'[9] Discovering your Truth of No Return can be harsh."

"Gandhi also said that it takes humility to face the truth," said the Financial Advisor.

"True," said the Guru. "We'll get to that. So, what are your truths?"

The Banker stared at the bar. The Financial Advisor fixed his gaze on the Guru, as though studying his bare head for answers. The Stockbroker picked at a nail.

"Would it help if I asked some questions?" the Guru finally said.

The communal sigh of relief was almost palpable. "Yes," said the Stockbroker. Of the three professionals, her armor had been the thickest and thorniest, but she had clearly been shaken from her defensive posture. She leaned forward on her elbows.

The Guru asked, "Why do you do what you do?"

It was as if he had asked a group of middle-school students to explain Keynesian economics. A hush fell over the small crowd.

"To make a living?" the Banker asked tentatively in a voice that belied his six-foot-one frame and lifeguard's build.

"That's one answer, but not the right one," the Guru said. "Let me be more precise with my language. What purpose are you serving with the work that you do?"

The atmosphere in the bar became truly funereal. This was a brain-scratcher. Patient and unflappable, the Guru slowly mixed and sipped his drink, never taking his eyes off his students and their deeply furrowed brows.

Finally, the Financial Advisor raised his hand. "To help my clients pick the best products."

The Guru slammed his drink down, making them all jump. "Pick the best products? What are you running, a grocery store? Annuities on aisle four, mutual funds on aisle seven, oh, and watch out, we have a nasty stock spill on aisle five! My friend, a monkey can pick products. If your entire purpose for doing what you do is to push product on clients, whether it's right for them or not, you are an enabler, not an advisor. If you are trying to sell someone, you will give him what he wants. If you are trying to serve him, you will give him what he needs.

"People know what they want; they don't know what they need," he continued. "In that way, they are exactly like you with your careers. You know the kind of life you want your work to help you create, but you don't know what you need to do to get it." He pointed to the Banker. "How are you going to get there?"

The Banker furrowed his brow. "Uh, by sharing my knowledge of banking and financial products with people and help them make better decisions," he said.

"Well, no," said the Guru. "Knowledge is not a sufficient path to action, because we can know all the facts in the universe yet still be largely driven to act out of fear or desire for comfort. Think about it this way: we've known in this country for years that eating too much saturated fat and obesity leads to heart disease and premature death, right? Yet we're the fattest nation on earth. Knowledge by itself doesn't change behavior." He paused to write something on the blackboard near the bar:

Education is not salvation.

The Guru went on. "All your knowledge can't help your clients make the right decisions, son. If knowledge was enough to deliver financial security, everybody with a Series 7 license would be independently wealthy. I trust you've noticed that's not the case."

The Banker chortled. "Um, yeah. I wish."

Questions, Questions

"Any other answers?" said the Guru.

"To keep our jobs." The Stockbroker rhythmically knocked her fist on the bar. "Let's be honest, that's what we all do. We slave to meet the goals that our managers set for us and to follow the rules and to make sure that no matter what, we do just enough not to get fired. Then we go home late, eat alone, and try to ignore the fact that in about 12 hours, we've got to do the same thing all over again. That's the treadmill I was talking about." She glared at the men. "You know it's true. Everybody works that way. Even the guys in the corner office do. They've just sold their souls for a higher price."

The Guru let out a whistle. "Pretty withering candor," he said. "Very good. Do you gentlemen agree with her assessment?"

After a long silence, the Financial Advisor said, "I guess I do. I feel like a hamster on a wheel most of the time. I want to give my clients the best advice I can, but I'm also expected to push products and hit my numbers—not necessarily by an outside boss but by the culture of the business and my own expectations. It's a complete contradiction. I feel sometimes like I'm putting over a swindle, not just on my clients but on my own ability to do my job in a way that means more than just meeting my numbers. Does that make sense?"

"It does to me, man." The Banker reached across the bar and picked up two glasses, then filled one with water from the beverage hose. "It's like you start out with this," and he pointed to the full glass of water, "being your inspiration, I guess, for doing your job in a certain way, according to a certain set of ethics or morals. Slowly, you fall into a pattern of running on automatic." He poured a little of the water into the empty glass, then a little more, and then still more. "And over time, your ability to do things for any other reason than 'That's the way I did them yesterday and the day before' disappears. You're just trying to play by the rules and stay out of trouble."

The Guru looked at all three for a long moment, and then raised his glass to them. "I think you're all very impressive. I'm delighted it was you who found your way here. Very astute introspection, all of you." He set down his drink, wandered over to the chalkboard, and erased what was written. "But not quite on the money. You're close, but you haven't gotten to the heart of your Truth of No Return yet."

"Wait a second," said the Financial Advisor. "You're talking like there is a single truth for all three of us, for everyone in the financial world. I thought each person's truth was supposed to be unique."

"It is unique in how it's expressed," said the Guru, "but think about it: how many unique truths about people are there? Not that many. Money doesn't buy happiness. You have to love yourself before you can love others. Do unto others as you would have them do unto you. These are universal truths that apply to everyone. It's just the circumstances that vary from person to person."

They took this in, sitting in silence.

The Pursuit of More

"It's a bit disturbing, isn't it, to think that the biggest crisis of your life might not be that different from that experienced by billions of others," the Guru said.

"Indeed it is," said the Financial Advisor.

"Doesn't matter," the Guru said. "What *does* matter is how you discover your truth and what you do with it. Your solution and your journey won't be the same as anyone else's. In fact, most people will never even look for their truth, much less do anything with it. You're already among the chosen few in that you're seeking. The trick is to finish the process."

"So finish it," said the Banker. "Clue us into what our Truth of No Return is, because I don't think we have any more guesses."

"Very well." The Guru took his chalk in hand and walked to the chalkboard. After wiping it clean, he carefully wrote:

The pursuit of more.

"More what?" asked the Stockbroker.

"More everything," said the Guru. "In *Good to Great*, Jim Collins writes about this concept, except he calls it the 'undisciplined pursuit of more.' It's primarily about money, because as author and business strategist Gary Hamel said, we live in a society that believes the size of the paycheck compensates for the quality of character.[10] Money is only part of it. In the end, we're after more for its own sake: more money, more prestige, more recognition, more impressive titles after our name, a more spacious office, more ways to wow our friends with our wealth and status, and so on. More, more, more, but with that endless pursuit comes an inherent slavery. You think you're free, but you know the thing about the guy who wrote 'all men are created equal' in the Declaration of Independence? He kept slaves. Everything has a price. Even self-actualization has a price."

"What's the price of self-actualization?" asked the Stockbroker.

"The death of all comforting self-delusion," the Guru said. "The price of more is that you become its slave, especially when the focus is money, which it almost always is. Lou Cassara says 'You can make money, or you can earn money.'[11] If your focus is on making money, you'll do whatever it takes. You'll compromise your principles, sell the latest products to your clients to grab a commission, and work 70-hour weeks even if it means never seeing your kids. Making more money is all about the short term, the quick fix. As long as more money is your goal, you'll continue making fear-based decisions and hating what you do."

"So are you against making money?" This was the Stockbroker, who was looking over the bar with a hard glint in her eye, as if daring the Guru to take a socialist stand against the bad capitalist beast.

He wasn't taking the bait. "Of course not. I said that before. There is nothing wrong with making money. There's just nothing good about it, either. It's a tool, that's all. It's about the *why*, remember? If you're in business for no other reason than to make money, you'll do anything to make more of it. That's where the theory of relativity comes in."

The Banker shook his head. "Say what? Now you're getting into physics, man. I'm totally confused."

"Not that theory of relativity," the Guru said. "This is the financial theory of relativity. I'm going to borrow your trick, good sir, to demonstrate." He grabbed the glasses of water that the Banker had used earlier and filled them, one half full and one three-quarters full, and then hid the three-quarters-full glass beneath the bar. "Let's say this glass is a

15 percent return on your portfolio. You'd be happy with that, right?"

"Are you kidding?" said the Financial Advisor. "That's a great return, especially considering historical averages."

"Right," said the Guru. "You think 15 percent would make you happy. Well, don't believe everything you think. If your focus is on the pursuit of more rather than on some larger meaning behind your work, guess what?" He brought the three-quarters-full glass into view. "The next year, the market is up 25 percent, but your investments again return 15 percent. Nothing has changed for you, but now you're unhappy. Why? Because you could have had MORE! You're not keeping up with relative performance, even though you know it's a short-term phenomenon and making radical changes in asset allocation to chase that higher performance could harm your clients and you in the long run. When more is all that matters, that's exactly what you'll do."

"Hey, we didn't make the rules," said the Stockbroker. She seemed to know it was an empty argument.

"True," the Guru said, "but who said you had to play by them? Chasing more is a very common human weakness. It's the brain at work again. When we receive more, we experience joy from a chemical called dopamine that's released into the brain. When we get a new car, it feels really great, but in about six months, we habituate to that new level of dopamine and the pleasure decreases. We want another car. We say, 'I need the newest model' or 'I need the Jaguar.' You buy it, get another dopamine surge, and in another six months, the feeling wears off and you think life can't continue unless you own a Ferrari. Just as a drug addict needs more and more to get high, so do we in our pursuit of more. It never stops. They say life is a journey, but when the only goal is the pursuit of more, it's a journey to nowhere, because we can never be satisfied.

"As we get more and more, we start to become more disillusioned," he continued. "We start to realize we're not happy—that something's wrong. Where is the eternal contentment that we were promised would be ours if we would only keep chasing after more? We don't find it, so we keep buying into the lie. Doing otherwise would mean admitting that the pursuit of more has been totally empty. We become ravenous for more, always starving, because there's never enough to satisfy our hunger. That's why suicide rates rise during economic downturns.[12] Some people spend years chasing the gold ring, and in the process, alienate their families and become strangers to their kids. When they lose so much, they realize that it was all a big lie and take a dive out a window."

The Inverse Square Law of Inspiration

The students sat with heads bowed, deep in thought.

The Guru ran his finger around the rim of a wine glass, trying for the characteristic musical ring of real crystal. "Seems I've struck a nerve," he said softly. "See, the thing is, there's a law at work here. You," he addressed the banker, "you seem familiar with physics, yes?"

"Took two years in college, sure," the Banker said.

"You're familiar then with the inverse square law of gravity, right? The force that gravity exerts on an object decreases according to the square of the distance the object is from the source of gravity. Well, here we're dealing with what I call the Inverse Square Law of Inspiration."

"What the hell is that?" asked the Banker, his surf-guy cool turning to intense interest.

"When you go back to the beginning of any business, including a financial services company, the person who started the company didn't do it only for money," the Guru said, leaning over the bar as he made his point. "He or she also started it because of passion. There was a powerful mission behind the company's launch: make banking more available to the middle class, help investors get better access to information, or who knows what. In any case, the company began on the bedrock of principle and passion." The Guru sat back on his stool. He seemed to be approaching some critical point.

"But as time goes by, and the people involved in the company get farther and farther away from that starting point, from the gravity of the founder's passion and mission, they care less and less. The reason for the company's existence becomes less about principle and more about money for money's sake, and that spirit infects everyone from the top down. The entire culture becomes about pursuing more for more's sake. Soon, the principles of the founder are completely forgotten. Just quaint artifacts of an irrelevant era." He crossed his legs. "Sound familiar?"

"Yes," said the Stockbroker. "It sounds like Wall Street in general. An entire culture built around next-quarter's earnings reports. We all play the game. I hate it more than I can say."

The Banker and Financial Advisor locked eyes with the woman, and the three of them silently realized that they shared an uncomfortable reality: they were willing participants in a system that used them up and spat them out.

The Financial Advisor turned back to the bar. "I guess we've discovered our brutal fact, haven't we?"

"Yes, you have," said the Guru. "Your Truth of No Return isn't just that your business has primarily become about nothing more than the ravenous chase of wealth. It's that you've willingly played a part in it, and it doesn't feel very good." He kicked his feet up and planted his biker boots on the bar, right in front of his startled students. "Of course, the tragic irony of it all is that all that selling out isn't the way to make more money anyway. The whole thing is a big, fat lie."

"What do you mean?" said the Banker.

"Well, Lou Cassara didn't just talk about making money, he also talked about *earning* money. You earn money by doing things that are right for others according to a set of values. If you make money but don't earn it, the universe has a way of taking it from you. When you earn the money, it supports your lifestyle and self-esteem."

Selling or Serving?

"That's what we refer to as character," the Guru went on. "We find that gifts come to people who have character, people who put mission and purpose above accruing wealth for its own sake. People who help others, work hard, and act with integrity often end up very successful. The trouble is that many of them, once they receive the gifts, are tempted to ditch character in order to keep the gifts. They let go of the very virtues that brought them the gifts—their mission, discipline and ethics—and every single time, those gifts are taken away. Then they're back to building character again through tough times when they have nothing. That's a cycle I wouldn't want to repeat."

"I've repeated it," said the Stockbroker. "Most of my clients have, too."

"But your main job is to prevent that from happening," said the Guru. "You're supposed to impose discipline on your clients by thinking long term and serving their needs, not your own. If you're in the business to sell, not to serve, you are destined to repeat that cycle again and again until you learn or have nothing left. Nobody wants to be on their deathbed surrounded by pictures of their boat, car, and big-screen TV."

"How big?" said the Banker. This earned him a glare from the other three. "Just kidding. Geez, lighten up."

"So you're saying that's the key to escaping the pursuit of more? Serving rather than selling?" asked the Financial Advisor.

"Bingo," said the Guru. "Truly successful people all serve something greater than their own personal interest. As a result, they developed the discipline, values, and passion that kept them doing the right things over many years and that made them wealthy in all the ways that matter: happiness, strong relationships, health, and financial security." He took his Yankees cap from the bar and dropped it back on his head, snugging it down as he made his point. "You should not be in your business to sell. That is not your primary value to others. You should be in your business to serve."

Tick tick tick . . . The broken clock kept time as the point sank in. Finally, the Stockbroker asked the question they were all thinking. "Serve what?"

"Ah," said the Guru. He walked to the other end of the bar, where a small office had been created, presumably for things like bookkeeping and storing records. Rummaging around in a drawer, he came away with a large black marker. He walked back to the center of the bar, leaned toward the long mirror, and wrote on it in block letters a foot high:

PURPOSE

"Isn't that vandalism?" said the Banker. By now, they were all comfortable gibing with the Guru.

"Wipes off," he shot back. "Purpose is the only thing you can serve. If you are doing your work without purpose, you are just a salesperson, and a salesperson is as much a sheep as any client off the street. Your knowledge won't make a difference. If you're serving something richer and higher, you'll make different decisions. You become the value, the person in your chair, not the product on the shelf. This gives you the freedom to break free of the cycle of more. Purpose makes you significant."

"Significant?" asked the Financial Advisor.

"Yes. Significance means making a long-term positive difference in the lives of the people you serve," the Guru said. "The most prominent financial deity can't do that if she or he is only serving the idea of more. 'Never confuse prominence with significance,' Rick Warren said. He also did this once in front of an audience to demonstrate—" The Guru pointed at the Roman nose protruding from his face. "'My nose is quite prominent, but it's not very significant.'"

They all chuckled.

"So the question I have to ask you is this: what purpose are you serving?" the Guru said, sitting down and clasping his hands together. "Lou Cassara wrote that who you are is more important than what you do. So maybe a better question is, what kind of person does your purpose make you?"

"What if we don't know our purpose?" asked the Financial Advisor.

"That's the whole point of being here," replied the Guru. "You've faced your Truth of No Return—that you're all part of this cyclical, empty pursuit of more. Bravo—and brava—to you for admitting that, but that's not enough. I shared with you a while back that you already know the life and career you want. Well, you all know your purpose as well. It's inside you, waiting to escape past the walls of cynicism and shame that you've erected around it. You just need to dig for it and bring it to the surface. That's what we're going to do next. Get your shovels."

Lesson Three

Becoming Purpose-Powered

"Sacrifice your familiar practices on the altar of higher purpose."

—*Gary Hamel*

"People align with others who share the same values."

—*Lou Cassara*

"The mere possession of a vision is not the same as living it, nor can we encourage others with it if we do not, ourselves, understand and follow its truths. The pattern of the Great Spirit is over us all, but if we follow our own spirits from within, our pattern becomes clearer. For centuries, others have sought their visions. They prepare themselves, so that if the Creator desires them to know their life's purpose, then a vision would be revealed. To be blessed with visions is not enough . . we must live them!"

—*High Eagle, Native American musician*

The Guru spoke confidently. "In Jonah Lehrer's book *How We Decide,* cognitive scientist Roger Shank says that when facts become widely available and instantly accessible, each one becomes less valuable. What begins to matter more is the ability to place these facts in context and to deliver them with emotional impact."

The Financial Planner was emerging from the men's room, wiping his hands on his pants, and heard the Guru utter this statement seemingly out of nowhere. "Holy non sequitur, Batman," he said. "What was that again?"

The Banker smiled. "Oh, I feel another lesson coming on."

The Guru glared at the Financial Advisor. "What, did they run out of towels in there? What would your mother say?"

The Financial Advisor took his seat. "She'd say I was considerate for not wasting trees when I have perfectly good pants to dry my hands on," he snapped. "I was raised by hardcore environmentalists. They are both still members of the Sierra Club. Old habits die hard, I guess."

"Ah, that's exactly my point," the Guru said. "Where is our fourth?"

The crack of billiard balls served as an answer. Across the room, standing with a pool cue propped by her side like the figure from Grant Wood's painting *American Gothic*, was the Stockbroker. She surveyed a formation of pool balls with a gimlet eye as she chalked up her stick. "Present and listening," she said. "Please go on."

"Thank you, I will," the Guru said. "My comment about Shank was intended to illustrate that abundance commonly creates meaninglessness. When we have no scarcity of something, it loses its context and becomes empty. It's true with information, and it's true with money." He sat back and lazily folded his hands behind his head, stretching. "You remember that we were talking about purpose. Well, you have faced your brutal Truth of No Return and admitted that you're in business for a reason that is destroying you and your future. The next task is to discover a spirit-nourishing reason to go to work each day—to find your purpose. Most of the people in your profession are purpose deficient. I'm going to teach you how to change that."

"That's a tall order." The Stockbroker slammed the seven-ball home with a crack of the cue. "I suppose earning a good living isn't purpose enough?"

"Nice shot, but you know that cue is a little warped, don't you?" the Guru said.

The Stockbroker shot back a small, sly smile. "I'm a little warped," she said. "It's a good match."

The Financial Advisor and Banker laughed. "Good answer," said the Banker.

He knitted his brows in thought before continuing while the Financial Advisor, Stockbroker, and Guru gave him silence. "I don't think that money, by itself, is a reason for anything. It's a result of work, but it's not a reason *for* it. The fact that so many of us are working only for money is what's got many of us going down a blind alley where there's never enough money, time, or satisfaction. I'd rather earn less and be satisfied with the quality of what I earn." The young man looked around, looking more than ever like a surfer who'd been poured into an expensive shirt and a silk tie. "Wow," he said.

"Nice speech," retorted the Guru, "and you are correct. Einstein said, 'Do not ask how to be a man of success, but set out to be a man of value.' The question is, what defines your value? What values define your value? In the end, people connect with others over shared values, not over service or money. Money isn't a value. It's a tool, but that seems to be the dead end for most financial pros. It's about what will make them the most money in the short term, even though it's been proven again and again that career longevity, personal satisfaction, and greater income come from adhering to a set of values that mean something to the people you're working with and hold you to a higher standard of behavior. In other words . . ." He erased the chalkboard again and wrote:

Your values determine your value.

Values under Pressure

The Financial Advisor had begun stacking cardboard beer coasters on the bar. He peered over a tower that was now about five inches high. "If that's true, why don't most of the people in our line of work pursue a values-based business?"

The Guru aimed a rugged finger at him. "Good question. Anyone want to answer it?" He looked around. "Anyone? Anyone? Bueller?" He cackled. "Sorry, I couldn't resist."

The Stockbroker clicked home the thirteen ball and stood straight. "Because it's hard, I suspect."

"Clarify, please," said the Guru.

She cocked her head. "Well, you'd have to swim upstream against the culture of your bank, brokerage, or broker-dealer. Many of them are all about short-term growth and rewarding whoever puts away the fattest commissions. There aren't a lot of junkets to Cabo San Lucas for registered reps and stockbrokers who turn away business that's not in tune with their values. Heck, I don't think most of my colleagues even know what their values are."

The Guru nodded vigorously. "That's right," he said, "and when you don't know your values and what you stand for, you can't know the purpose you serve with your work. If you have a purpose aligned with your values, that becomes the most important reason for the choices you make, no matter what kind of pressure your company or culture puts on you. If not, you're basically a slave serving an ever-escalating need for more and more and more. That is the difference between being a fiduciary and an enabler."

The Banker looked up sharply. "Say what?"

"Barbara Roper is the director of investor protection for the Consumer Federation of America. She said that her federation's surveys show that the majority of people who work with a financial advisor trust that they're getting good advice," the Guru said.[13] "She also said that 'to be that trusting outside of a situation where a person is committed to putting your interests first is pretty risky business.' A financial professional who is committed to putting his or her clients' interests first is a fiduciary, someone legally and ethically bound to advise clients on the path that best serves their long-term wealth, even if it costs the professional some short-term income. You know this, right?"

"Of course," said the Financial Advisor. "In the financial world, there are only three job titles that automatically connote a fiduciary standard: attorney, CPA, and Registered Investment Advisor. In those professions, you are obligated to put your clients first always, but in theory, even if you're not legally bound by a code of conduct, we're always supposed to do that."

"Uh-huh," said the Guru. "In theory, but how often does that happen in practice? How many of your colleagues practice that? How often have you three gone against your own self-interest to do what's in the client's interest?" He gazed around for an eye that would meet his and found no takers. "I don't want to tar the entire field," he continued. "There are some advisors, brokers, and bankers who are practicing their values and doing business the way it should be done. I think a lot more intend to do it that way, but I trust you all recall what is said to be paved with good intentions."

Finally, the Banker looked up. "We try," he said simply.

"Not good enough," snapped the Guru, "because the next word in that sentence is 'but,' as in, 'but there's just so much pressure,' or 'but I have a car payment to make.' That's the inevitable result of a working life driven by the brain's need for short-term pleasure and the avoidance of pain. When you come to work every day with a purpose that serves your values, nothing can ever exert enough pressure to overcome your desire to live up to those values. It transforms how you see yourself and what you do. Otherwise, you're just an enabler."

"What exactly do you mean by that?" the Stockbroker said from across the room.

"I'll show you." The Guru hopped over the bar in one amazingly agile move, brushing but not topping the Financial Advisor's foot-tall stack of coasters. He walked over to the pool table, chose a cue from the rack on the wall with careful consideration, and began to chalk it with the practiced ease of someone who has done his time in a thousand roadside dives in a thousand towns. "Let's put together a little example, shall we? Rack 'em, would you my dear?"

The Stockbroker hesitated and looked at the Banker and Financial Advisor for support. They both shrugged. She fished the triangular rack from beneath the table, corralled the pool balls, set the eight ball at the center, and expertly rolled the formation into place on one end of the green felt. The stained-glass Budweiser lamp threw amber light over the table; motes of blue chalk swirled in the air. The two men sauntered over, feeling that a new stage of this encounter was about to begin.

Fiduciary or Enabler?

"Thank you," said the Guru. He bent over and lined up his break. "Now, we're going to talk about the difference between clients and customers. See, one of the unique things about the game of pool is that it has a memory, just like Blackjack." The cue shot forward in a blur. The cue ball rocketed toward the formation of colored balls. Balls flew in all directions; three sunk into the pockets. What remained looked like a solar system of scattered planets.

"Nice break," said the Financial Advisor.

"Thank you. Each action or decision affects future decisions. Each ball on the table, the availability of each shot, and the ultimate outcome of the game is dependent on the position of all the others. Pool is an interdependent SYS-tem!" He fired the cue ball at the solid two ball, which ricocheted at an angle into the left corner pocket. "In *The Seven Habits of Highly Effective People*, Steven Covey says that we go from dependence as babies to independence as adult, but Covey said 'there is one more stage, and that's interdependence, making ourselves accountable to others.' That's what a fiduciary relationship should be. The financial professional and the client meet over a shared set of values, work collaboratively, and mutually understand that what best serves the long-term interests of the client also serves the long-term interests of the professional."

He took aim at a cluster of balls and shot. One ball banked up against the rim of the pocket but didn't fall. "Your shot," the Guru said to the Stockbroker. He pointed at the Banker. "You're on my team."

"Um, okay," the Banker said.

The woman walked around the table, eyeing striped balls and possible shots. "I don't understand where the client-customer difference comes in. Call me obtuse." She sent a ball across the length of the table and sank it.

"I'd call that a nice shot," said the Financial Advisor.

"Look at the definitions of the words," the Guru said, standing and slowly twirling his cue between his fingers. "The dictionary defines customer as someone who buys goods and services from another. It's a transaction, nothing more, but a client is defined as a person or group that uses the professional advice or services of another. A relationship is implied. More important than that, the value of the service provider is implied. I don't know if I'd take that shot, ma'am." He nodded at the difficult bank shot that the Stockbroker seemed to be lining up.

She rifled her cue through her tented fingers as she eyed the shot. "Thank you." The cue flashed forward; the ball nicked the felt rail and dropped neatly into the hole across the table. "I'll keep that in mind."

The Guru grinned broadly. "I think we have a ringer. I wouldn't have guessed you were so skilled, young lady."

Her bravado melted into a slender smile. "I had a boyfriend during college who rode a Harley. We cruised all over the Midwest and hung out in a lot of bars. I learned to play as a survival skill. We broke up when I got better than him." She missed a table-length bank shot. "Damn. You're up," she said to the Banker.

He took the cue from the Guru. "I, on the other hand, am not very good at this, but since it's a metaphor or something, I'll give it a go." He surveyed the table. "What did you mean—the value of the service provider is implied? You're talking about us."

The Guru watched over the young man's shoulder as he perused his shot options. "Let's look at it this way," he said, "if you're playing partners pool, you can play the game one of two ways. You can fire away for your own glory, chasing impossible shots even when you know you can't make them, or you can make choices that will set up your partner while hindering your opponents. In other words, you can think only of yourself or of the interdependent whole. Which do you think makes for a more satisfying experience?"

He finished as the Banker sent the cue ball careening across the table into the six ball, which jostled around and finally sank into a side pocket. "Yes!" the Banker cried, high-fiving his partner.

"See," continued the Guru, "if you had missed that shot, you would have left your pal here, our adversary, with a gimme in the corner. That's what I'm talking about, but perhaps I need to be clearer. In your various businesses, you sell product, right?"

"True," replied the Financial Advisor, already thinking ahead to his shot.

"Fine. Product providers sometimes use fear to sell you on selling their financial products, and the core fear they use is that you aren't good enough. Their often-unconscious goal is to make you feel that you are only as good as your products. Since their product is the best, by that logic if you sell it to your clients, now you're the best, but people who only buy products are not clients; they're customers. They're not looking for expertise or behavior modification or to have discipline enforced upon them. They're looking for an enabler who will give them what they want when they want it, be that buying when the market is high or selling when it is low. If you have customers, not clients, you're nothing more than an order taker."

Bam! The cue ball jumped the rail and hit the floor with a crash, startling the entire group, except for the Guru, who watched serenely as the Financial Advisor chased the ball. "Sorry," said the Banker. "I told you I wasn't very good."

"Doesn't matter, man," said the Financial Advisor as he placed the ball on one of the table's center markers. He looked at the Guru. "So you're saying that being in the business just to make money can lead to being just an order taker . . . an enabler?"

"That's right," said the Guru. "Clients don't buy competence as much as they buy confidence. They see your excitement about a product as confidence, and that is what they buy—your confidence. They assume that behind your belief in a product lies a core of values and character, and those are really what they buy. They assume that if your values drive you to care about the same things they care about, you will give them advice that will get them closer to what they care about. Customers, on the other hand, just want to be enabled. They want you to say yes to their most short-sighted, self-destructive choices, and if you're an enabler, that's what you'll do, because it's largely about making the sale and getting the commission."

"I have to admit—" the Financial Advisor paused to angle a shot into the corner pocket. He fired and sank the ball. "That's what most of my colleagues do. They're out for the immediate financial gain, and they pay little mind to what's in the best interest of the customer."

"Let's not be self-righteous here," said the Stockbroker. "We all do it. We all play the game to some extent, make the compromises. We all convince ourselves that we're being fiduciaries when we're often being enablers, and in the process we deny ourselves the kinds of clients we can keep for 30 years."

The Financial Advisor slowly drew back his cue stick and fired a shot across the table, aiming the ball toward the corner pocket. It rattled around in the corner before rolling out.

"Mmm," said the Guru. "See, you set me up perfectly, which you didn't want to do." He quickly shot home a solid ball. "None of you get it yet. This isn't just about your practices and your business relationships. This is about you, personally. About whether you're going to thrive in what you've chosen to do or if it's going to ruin you."

Coming to the Office in Fear

He blew chalk dust from his fingers and measured off a cross-table shot.

"What?" This was the Banker. "What do you mean?"

"I mean—" a ball slid home quietly as he continued, "—that this is about you and all those in your profession who are robbing themselves of their empowerment while they give their customers exactly what they don't need. You don't seem to understand that you all come to the office in a subconscious state of fear every single day and spend each day denying that fear. It doesn't have to be that way. If you find your true worth in something other than the money you make, you can have purpose in what you do and, at the same time, build an incredible practice that will make you rich in more ways than you can imagine.

"Psychologist Stephen Hayes said that people use behavioral rules to control their conduct when they might otherwise fall under the spell of the moment," he continued. "Well, people may use self-talk to temper their behavior in many ways, but when it comes to money, they often feel the end justifies the means. Money for the sake of money has no end, so all you're left with is the means, and the means become your end. If your means are without character you're left with money and no character. The trade-off is misery and disillusionment."

"That's Howard Hughes." The Banker looked up, waiting for a response. When it didn't come, he pushed on. "Basing your self-worth on your financial worth. That's what he did, aside from the obsessive-compulsive disorder. What you're saying, I think, is that we're letting our desire for money influence the value we find in what we do. Right?"

The Guru barely missed a difficult deflection shot. "So close," he said, "and so close. You're very close but not quite on the money. It's about fear. The system you have sold yourself to has convinced you that the only valid measure of your worth is the amount of money you make. When you come to the office each day, you're coming to the office in fear. From this emotion and state of mind, you can end up pushing products that people don't need. You deny your own character out of the fear that you won't make the short-term dollars that prove your self-worth. You're all on that endless product-pushing treadmill to the grave, because you've bought the lie that your purpose is nothing more than creating revenue. You stay on the treadmill because you're selling yourselves short. Deep down, you believe that the lie might be true. Well, let me share this with you."

He took the blue pool chalk and wrote on the small board that players used to keep score from game to game:

You cannot serve people or your purpose when you are in fear.

There was a long silence before the Stockbroker clicked home a striped ball with a graceful shot. "Nonsense," she said, like a judge passing down a sentence, "I don't work out of fear."

"Of course you do." The Financial Advisor was standing about 10 feet away with a cluster of darts in his hand, perhaps intimidated by the skill of the Guru and the Stockbroker. He threw a dart at a worn dartboard about six paces distant. *Thock*—nearly a bull's-eye. "Nearly everyone I know in my business has a passion for what they do, but they bury that passion because they're afraid of not making their numbers. We all try to be shepherds, not sheep, but most of us make at least some short-sighted recommendations and compromise people's interests because we're afraid of not making enough money."

The Stockbroker blasted the cue ball with a hard stroke— it bounded past the men and across the floor, then crashed through the window and tumbled into the street. She didn't notice. "There's nothing wrong with making money!" she shouted.

The Guru walked over to inspect the window. "Never said there was. Hmm, going to have to call the insurance company about that one." He returned to the pool table, where the young woman glowered while the Banker glanced back and forth between her and the Guru. "What I've been saying is that money cannot be your purpose in doing what you do. It cannot be your why. Let's talk about money for a second. You'd all like to make more, right? How do you do it? Many people would say that you consistently recommend the best funds and the best products, but then why should a client choose you, if you turn them into a customer? 'Here, put your money in this,' you tell them. A monkey can do that. In fact, a monkey named Mr. Adam Monk has done that for the *Chicago Sun-Times* since 2003 and has consistently beaten the market.[14]

"You don't build something extraordinary by shoving product at people because you're afraid NOT to shove it at them," the Guru continued, standing with his hands clasped in the center of the three younger people. "You do it by inspiring them with actions driven by your character and your values. Those qualities come from knowing the purpose that you serve. People are inspired by values. Even the most cynical man has a secret place in his heart where something moves him—honesty, compassion, courage, something. When you reach that place, you've got a client for life."

First Principles

"Fabulous," snapped the Stockbroker, setting down her cue. It was unclear if she was expressing her disgust over the premature end of the game, the Guru's comments, or both. "That's a wonderful thought, but we have to work in the real world. There, you've got to make your numbers and pay your Visa® bill. Principle and inspiration are luxuries."

Thock. The Financial Advisor threw another dart. "No," he said. "He's right."

"Excuse me?" the Stockbroker replied.

"Just sit down for a second and listen, please."

The Guru hopped up onto the bar to see where his pupils would take the discussion.

The Financial Advisor took a place on a barstool while the Banker inspected his own set of darts. "A few years back, an advisor that I knew told me a story. He'd had someone come to his office wanting investment advice. The gentleman was a retired college professor, and he had a retirement account with a balance of about $300,000. Well, my friend told me that the professor was getting a very nice return on his money. He asked my friend, 'What do you recommend I do with the $300,000 sitting in this fixed rate account?' This advisor thought about it and replied, 'There are few guarantees in life, and that's an impressive one. I recommend you stay where you are.' You know what the prospect said? 'I have found my advisor.' He then told my buddy that he had met with four other advisors, and every single one of them wanted him to move the account. He told my friend, 'I will keep this account where it is, based on your recommendation, but because I feel you are the only one who has been honest with me, I have another $500,000 that I want you to invest.'"

"Wow," said the Banker.

"True story?" said the Stockbroker.

"Absolutely."

"That's a perfect example of what I'm talking about," said the Guru, hauling himself off the bar. "That's values-driven behavior. Your friend was serving, not selling."

The Banker tossed his own dart and missed the board entirely. "Oops. That's great, but that sort of client doesn't come along every day, you know."

The Guru shook his head. "Doesn't matter. The point is that you can't wait for the type of client who comes in your door in order to change the fulcrum on which your career moves," he said. "Marcus Aurelius talked about first principles. Do any of you know what that means?"

Thock. The Financial Advisor had pierced the bull's-eye with his dart. "Don't look at me," he said. "I'm planning my future as a professional dive bar darts champion." The Stockbroker looked at the floor.

"I've read Aurelius," said the Banker. "'Examine the matter from first principles, from this: If all things are not mere atoms, it is nature which orders all things: if this is so, the inferior things exist for the sake of the superior, and these for the sake of one another.'[15] He means that to understand something, you have to go to its essential nature, to its origin." He wandered over to the bar.

"My goodness, you're hiding quite the Renaissance man beneath that boyish exterior, my friend," said the Guru, and the Banker ducked his head with a grin. "Yes. First principles means that you set aside all the outcomes, choices, and interpretations of a situation and look only at the prime mover of events. The prime mover of your practice is you. You have to change the purpose for your work without worrying about the clients that will be drawn to it and make new choices that are motivated by your values and character. The rest will take care of itself."

The Stockbroker stood. "That sounds like New Age bunk," she said.

"It may, but it's not. It's human nature, a first principle," the Guru replied.

"I can't base my entire practice on that," she said crossly.

"Why not?"

She was silent.

Where Does Your Worth Come From?

The Guru took up the final set of darts and stepped between the two younger men to face the dartboard. He threw a dart. *Thock*. Bull's-eye. "You can't do it because you believe the lie that your value is based primarily on money," he said. "We live in a country where we use the word *worth* to describe both our financial worth and self-worth. That's dangerous, because we inevitably equate the two.

"If you live under the illusion that you're not worthy, you will depend on that which you sell and you will define yourself by what you do," he continued. "Often in our culture, when we become *worth less*, we become worthless in our own eyes. That's why people who lose everything financially often commit suicide. They base their worth on money and when it's gone, they believe they have no value. Man makes the money, but the money should NOT make the man."

Thock. Another perfect shot.

"Okay, I think you get to be the darts professional, and I'll just be your corner man," said the Financial Advisor. He turned to the Banker, eyebrows raised. The Banker grinned from behind the bar and poured a drink.

The Stockbroker walked over and stuck a finger into the Guru's chest. "My worth is not just about the money I make," she said through her teeth.

The Guru was the picture of calm. Gently, he said, "Then where does your worth come from?"

"I . . ." She turned on her heel and walked to the other side of the bar by the jukebox.

"Same question for all of you," the Guru went on. "Where does your worth come from? Does it come from what you earn and what you do? Or from who you are and what you serve?" As if on cue, Stevie Ray Vaughan's "The Sky Is Crying" blared from the jukebox. "We're into deep territory now. Self-worth, values, and purpose are all tightly linked. Like the song "Love and Marriage" says, you can't have one without the other. Everything, and I mean everything, starts from the same place." He walked behind the bar, behind the Banker, and wrote with the black marker on the mirror:

Know where your worth comes from for your clients, your family, and yourself.

The Banker shook his head. "You've lost me, bro."

The Guru sat back down on his seat behind the bar. "Let's try this. Are you all familiar with Joseph Campbell's description of The Hero's Journey?"

Nods all around.

"Good! You know that the hero embarks on a journey of self-discovery, loses everything, and reaches a point of dire extremity—and only at that point does he or she find the awareness to see true power. Well, that's the journey you're all on. Let me tell you about someone I once knew."

The Stockbroker, her shoulders slumped, walked over and sat next to the Banker. The Financial Advisor remained standing but turned away from the dartboard to listen.

"There was a man in your profession," the Guru said to the Financial Advisor, "who was very successful on the surface. He had the high income, the big car, the professional status, but inside, he was a scared, angry little boy. Turns out this man's father had walked out on his family. When the man was only 11 years old, living in Alabama, his family went on a vacation to Florida. He didn't know—couldn't have known—that he would never return to his home. On that trip, his father came to him in the wee hours one night, woke him, and said, 'Son, I'm sorry but Daddy has to leave.' And just like that, his father was gone. Abandoned his family on the spot."

"Poor kid," said the Banker softly.

"The kid grew into a man," the Guru went on, "and he studied psychology because he thought if he could figure out why people act the way they do, he would never be hurt again. He kept everyone and everything at arm's length. One ex-girlfriend sent him a card that said, 'I hope you have an efficient Christmas.' Another told him, 'You don't feel feelings, you do feelings,' but he didn't understand. Eventually he went into the financial industry, wholesaling products to financial advisors. He was arrogant, cocky, and scared to death. He pushed and pushed to be the best, but it wasn't so much because he wanted the money. It was because he was terrified of being a loser, like he perceived his father to be. For 33 years, he labored under the fear that his worth was defined by the numbers—by how well he avoided not becoming something he dreaded.

"He married at age 36, and within a year he was in therapy to save his marriage. The problem was simple and monstrous: his marriage and his career could not coexist when the first principle for both was his terror of not being successful enough. He had a new house, was building a lake house, and was wholesaler of the year, and he thought this all made him successful. Then his wife gave birth to their first son prematurely. He began to realize that he was an utter failure in what mattered most: his purpose, which was to serve his family and be the best man he could be, not the best wholesaler. His defining moment was when his wife said, 'You are in the room physically, but you are not here mentally.'"

The Stockbroker shook her head. "This isn't an unusual story in our business. I've seen many a family sacrificed on the altar of more."

"True," said the Guru, "but this man had a wife with the guts to start therapy on her own. He resisted until he realized that she was being the brave one and he the coward, so he started therapy on his own. It didn't go well at first. He was still too egotistical, too obsessed with the status of being a top salesman, and his pursuit of more, to see his fear. Then his grandfather, a Pentecostal minister, passed away. This had been the man's hero, and the greatest and richest person he had ever known. Yet his grandfather had no material wealth when he died. He worked as a mechanic and used every cent he earned to build churches throughout Texas. After the man spoke at his grandfather's eulogy, a young woman came up to him and said, 'If it weren't for your grandfather, my dad would be in Hell.' Talk about humbling. Talk about a life of service. The scales finally fell from the younger man's eyes. He had everything and yet he had done nothing. His grandfather had had virtually nothing, yet he had done everything.

"The man continued therapy with a life coach but from a new perspective: honesty and humility about the meaninglessness of what he had thought so meaningful," the Guru continued. "And 33 years after his father left, the son reached out to the father. They had dinner. They connected. They exchanged e-mails that ranged from angry to brutally honest. The man felt he finally understood that his father had not been a loser. He had done exactly what his son had been doing: attaching his worth to something that had no meaning. His son was a chip off the old block. They both had to learn humility and discover what they were serving before they could find the courage to reconnect. Today, father and son are firmly in each other's lives, and the man and his wife have been married 10 years and counting."

Serving or Selling?

A hush fell over the room. The fluorescent light over the bar buzzed. The trio seemed to be taking the story in.

The Financial Advisor threw another dart. *Thock.*

Finally, the Banker spoke up. "I knew a guy, a 38-year-old father of three. He jumped out of a window on the 17th floor of a building in New York. He threw his chair out the window and then jumped to his death. He was a hotshot in commercial banking, but here's the thing that haunts me: his kids didn't give a flying toot about his portfolio. They just loved their daddy. What could make a guy not care about never seeing his kids again?" Thin tears rolled down his boyish face.

"The same force that drove the father in my story to abandon his family," said the Guru. "Fear. When we start to find our value in our stuff and our accomplishments, we're confusing worth and value. We're confusing what we do and what we earn with who we are and what we serve, and the two are NOT equal."

"I've felt like that." The Banker's eyes burned from the other side of the bar. "I've felt like what I did didn't matter, like I was getting up in the morning for all the wrong reasons."

"So have I," said the Financial Advisor, strolling back to the bar with one dart in his fist. "I've had days when I can barely remember who I am, and that I have a wife and a daughter. I have felt like nothing matters except my quarterly numbers, and that when I don't make them, I don't matter and I HATE IT!" He slammed the single dart deep into the wood of the bar, where it quivered like a tiny Excalibur, sunk an inch deep in varnished oak.

"Nice work. We're going to get hit with a bill for repairs to this place," said the Stockbroker, "between that and the hole in the wind—" She stopped short, looking at the spot where the cue ball had crashed through the window into the street. The glass was as intact as if nothing had happened. "But wait . . . that ball cut right through the pane." She turned to the Guru. "You saw it, didn't you?"

He shrugged. "Did I?" He waved the Stockbroker over. She sat down at the bar. "Do you feel the same way they do?"

A nod.

"The reason you and most of your colleagues feel this way is because you have pinned your worth on how fast you run on the hamster wheel. Your values and sense of purpose are shaped by short-term thinking, motivated by the fear that if you don't make money, you are worthless. As long as financial professionals continue to do this, you will suffer, your clients will lose, and our culture will endure an endless, destructive cycle of booms and busts." He leaned forward with both palms on the bar. "Right now, your profession is largely about selling. If you want to get off the wheel, you must figure out what purpose you serve."

"But how can we change horses in midstream?" asked the Financial Advisor. "Our companies would bury us."

The Guru shook his head. "Only if you didn't eventually produce even greater results. Most financial pros think that they are in the business of high returns or selecting the best fund or security, because that's what the populace identifies as their value. Most advisors are often scapegoats for the bad decisions of their clients, but who lets them make those decisions? That's the enabling relationship that you can't allow. You might make the sale today, but it may cost you your practice tomorrow. Believe me, when your practice originates from service and rises to something higher and better, you will attract clients, not customers. You will create long-term relationships based on long-term discipline and trust. You will do better by your clients and yourself by becoming the value they seek." He went to the chalkboard again and wrote:

The value comes from the character and purpose of the person in your chair.

"So," and the Guru leaned on his elbows, "are you selling or serving?"

"How do we know?" asked the Banker, adding to the still-standing stack of beer coasters.

The Financial Advisor plucked a coaster from the tower and flicked it across the room. "I suspect that if you . . ." he began.

"You're serving if you're one pool ball among many on the table." This was the Stockbroker, who stared intensely at the Guru. "You're making decisions based on a greater mission that benefits everyone. Right?"

"Something like that," said the Guru. "Service means your choices and your recommendations to your clients are guided by a compass that's about something other than short-term, feel-good profit. Your true north is a value that's more important to you than anything, a purpose that defines who you are. You must become powered by purpose, not profit, and profit will take care of itself." He eyed the Financial Advisor. "What purpose do you serve?" He turned to stare back at the Stockbroker. "What purpose do you serve?" His eyes turned to the Banker. "And you."

The Banker held the older man's gaze. "I don't know," he said. "Taking care of people's futures?"

"Sounds like a greeting card," the Guru shot back. "Try again."

"Helping people enjoy what they value most," offered the Stockbroker.

"Not bad, but still off."

"Making people's time as valuable as possible," said the Financial Advisor. "Because time is more valuable than money."

The Guru lifted an eyebrow. "Continue."

"Well, you can always get more money," the Financial Advisor said, "but you can't ever get more time. Most people have it backward, like time is limitless and money is scarce. Maybe it's my job to help them reverse that."

Tough Questions

"There is no right answer, children," the Guru said softly, "but you're at least asking the questions of yourself, and that's the key. Questions are the enemy of complacency. Once we wake up and start asking questions that don't have simple answers, we've crossed the Rubicon, the point of no return. There's no erasing that new awareness, even though it might be disturbing or cause you regret."

He reached beneath the bar, pulled out a towel, wet it, and walked to the mirror, which was covered with his black marker scribbling. "I want you to keep asking the questions, even after we leave this place. You might not figure out the purpose that you serve right away—it's a huge question—but keep looking, because the answer defines who you are and who you're becoming, and it will determine the future of your practice and your life." He wiped away the writing on the mirror, took up the marker, and spent 15 minutes writing something new, a list of questions:

Why do your clients need you?
Are you happy?
How do you improve your clients' lives?
What do you think people in your profession should bring to the lives of their clients?
Are the people in your life proud of what you do?
Are you proud of your behavior toward loved ones?
What is most important to you?
What will you stand up for and what will you never stand for?
Have you sacrificed your passion to pursue wealth?
What would others say about your worth? What would you like them to say?
When someone at a party asks you about yourself, what is the first thing you tell them about: your material wealth or personal accomplishment?
What is the meaning of success for you?
Is your practice today bringing you closer to that kind of success?
What do you want people to say about you at your funeral?
Do you delude yourself?
Do you think others would agree with your answer?
What is your worth?

The Guru finished, flexing his hand.

"Your hand must be sore, man," said the Banker.

"Not as sore as my brain from just thinking about all those questions," said the Financial Advisor.

The Guru walked to the small office area and returned with three sheets of paper and three pencils. "Write them down," he ordered. "I don't want to have given myself arthritis for nothing."

They started writing, and the Stockbroker looked up. "You know, I wonder if we can really do this. Change how we do things, I mean. We're all so indoctrinated into the culture."

The Guru smiled softly. "You're less susceptible to outside influence than you realize. You've heard of subliminal advertising, right?" They nodded. "The term was coined by a gent named James Vicary, who conducted an experiment in a New Jersey movie theater in 1957. He placed a device that projects an image for a very short time in the projection booth and then during a showing of the movie *Picnic* shot messages like "Drink Coca-Cola®" and "Eat Popcorn" onto the screen for 1/3000th of a second at a time. Afterward, he revealed that the theater had seen an 18.1 percent jump in Coca-Cola sales and a 57.8 percent jump in popcorn purchases. There began the myth that subliminal advertising could *program* consumer behavior."

"Myth?" said the Banker.

"Vicary lied about his results," the Guru said. "He confessed that he had falsified his data. He couldn't get the same results when he repeated it. In fact, some people doubt whether he ever conducted the initial New Jersey experiment at all." The Guru spread his arms wide. "We're not computers. We're not programmable. We have choice."

"Which of course means we can't slough off responsibility either," said the Stockbroker.

"Bingo," said the Guru.

"But at least we're free to screw up," said the Financial Advisor.

"Yes you are," said the Guru, "and free to forgive yourself as well. Serving is a path of personal freedom because doing the right thing—focusing on values and character—

becomes its own reward," said the Guru. "Doing the right thing is where we're headed next."

The trio continued writing.

PART II
THE TRIANGLE OF TRUTH

Lesson Four

Faith Over Force

"When you have come to the edge of all light that you know and are about to drop off into the darkness of the unknown, faith is knowing one of two things will happen: There will be something solid to stand on or you will be taught to fly."

—*Patrick Overton*

"Faith is taking the first step even when you don't see the whole staircase."

— *Martin Luther King, Jr.*

"Have the courage to say no. Have the courage to face the truth. Do the right thing because it is right. These are the magic keys to living your life with integrity."

—*W. Clement Stone*

"Physics 101—" the Guru announced from the doorway of the bar's storage room. A half-hour had gone by, and the trio had been laboring over their lists of questions like high school students desperate to pass the year's exit exam and escape to summer vacation.

They looked whipped, defenses down. The Stockbroker's brittle façade of suit, severe rimmed glasses, and sharp red nails had cracked; glasses and jacket sat in a pile on a tabletop, and one nail had broken off as she chewed her pencil. The Banker had reverted to frat boy and shed his shoes; his feet were up on a table, toes flexing. The Financial Advisor had given into boredom and constructed an edible chessboard out of saltines, maraschino cherries, and more cocktail olives retrieved from the back room. He hunched over it, either contemplating a move or trying to prevent the Banker from eating his creation.

At the Guru's voice, they all turned. "—tells us that for every force there is an opposite, equal force. When a rocket's engine fires, the force of the engine's discharge isn't actually pushing the rocket into space. The rocket is pushing the Earth away, because the laws of inertia say that it must. The world operates on the force mentality: if you want something, you have to force it to come to you. Force is fear-based. Force is selling. Force is giving people what they want instead of what they need."

The three professionals stared. It was clear that they were becoming tired as much from listening as from the emotional examination of their fears and failures. The Guru smiled and sat down at one of the bar tables, lifting his booted feet onto one of the chairs. "Okay," he said, "let's dial it down a notch. Story time. Once upon a time there was a gardener who grew an enormous carrot."

"You're kidding, right?" The Financial Advisor eyed his chessboard. "Fairy tales?"

"Life is a fairy tale, son," the Guru replied. "This is from the book *The Prodigal God* by Timothy Keller. Listen and you might learn something." He stretched and continued. "Anyway, gardener, enormous carrot. So he took it to his king and said, 'My lord, this is the greatest carrot I've ever grown or ever will grow. Therefore I want to present it to you as a token of my love and respect for you.' The king was touched and discerned the man's heart. As the man turned to go, the king said, 'Wait! You are clearly a good steward of the earth. I own a plot of land right next to yours. I want to give it to you as a gift so that you can garden it all.' The gardener was amazed and delighted and went home rejoicing, but there was a nobleman at the king's court who overheard all this. He thought, 'My! If that is what you get for a carrot, what if you gave the king something better?'

"The next day the nobleman came before the king, and he was leading a handsome black stallion," the Guru went on. "He bowed low and said, 'My lord, I breed horses, and this is the greatest horse I've ever bred or ever will. Therefore I want to present it to you as a token of my love and respect for you.' The king discerned his heart, said thank you, took the horse, and dismissed him. The nobleman was perplexed. The king said, 'Let me explain. That gardener was giving me the carrot, but you were giving yourself the horse.'"

"Word," the Banker said.

"This is more about serving instead of selling, isn't it?" asked the Stockbroker.

"Precisely," said the Guru. "With that in mind, I want to tell you all something very important. I'm trying to open your minds, but I'm not trying to sell you on what I'm saying. Do you understand what I mean by that?"

After a moment, the Financial Advisor looked up. "I think you're saying that you're here to open the door, but it's up to us to walk through," he said. "Right?"

"Just like in *The Matrix*," said the Guru, laughing. "That's partially right, but it's more than that. You've heard the phrase *devil's advocate*? It means someone who's compelled to argue for the opposite view and point out all the ways things can go wrong. What would you say if someone told you they were an *angel's advocate*?"

The Stockbroker shook her head, making her earrings jingle. "Wait, would that be someone who points out all the ways that something can go right?"

The Guru leveled a lean finger at her. "That's exactly it. What's so wrong about that? We figure if someone talks about what can go right, they must be naïve or ignorant. Why?

Because the whole idea of incentive in our culture is based largely on fear: if you don't do this, your child won't get into a good college. If you don't buy this financial product you'll be eating cat food when you retire. If you don't take this drug, you'll have a heart attack by age 55. See? The angel's advocate fights a constant battle against self-interest that uses fear as its weapon."

He leaned forward, his face serious. "Bob Dylan sang, 'You don't need a weatherman to know which way the wind blows.' I'm not here to tell you which way the wind is blowing; you know it already. You're smart. The people in your profession are smart. That's not the problem. The problem is that knowing isn't enough, and I'm going to talk about that later, but it's important that you understand this—if I was trying to sell you on this knowledge, I would be doing it so that you would validate me and approve of my wisdom. It would be about a reward for myself. If I wanted to sell you on these ideas, I would tell you about all the ways they would benefit you financially or materially. That would be focusing on myself, because you would then think of me as wise. That isn't the path. It's fine to benefit from your work; otherwise, why work? But financial and material benefit shouldn't be the only reason you serve. The farmer who grew the carrot didn't need the king's approval to affirm the worth of what he did. He got joy and reward from the process of creating something of beauty and value. It wasn't about the result. It was about the path. You can be about the result in part as long as you're also about the path. The path is about being what the sociologist David Riesman calls 'other directed.'"

Sailboat Success

They were all paying close attention—chins resting on hands, eyes fixed on their teacher.

"We're told that if we do this or that, we will be worthy," he continued. "Usually it involves making a certain amount of money or acquiring certain material objects. The truth is that we are worthy because of who we are, not what we do. My goal is to show you a better way to be, because that is its own reward. It's the true path to success in the greatest definition of the word. I'm not trying to sell you. I'm here to serve you so you can serve others. As Victor Frankl said, 'Success will follow you precisely because you have forgotten to think of it.'"

The Stockbroker raised her hand like a child in school. "So if we set our minds to being better, in terms of following our purpose and serving others, we will end up doing better?"

"Yes."

"For many people, that's going to be a tough sell, sir." She crossed her arms defensively. "The financial world can be pretty jaded."

The Guru stood up. "I know," he said. "Our entire society, and your entire profession, is primarily built around short-term thinking and the concept that to be more, you must do more. Contrary to the values you've been taught, there are two kinds of success. There is what I call *powerboat success*, which has nothing to do with a powerboat. It means that your success is built on something that has a limited life and can easily be taken away from you. If you have a powerboat, it's only a useful as the fuel in the tank. Take away the fuel, and the boat is basically a buoy. Powerboat success is success based on material things that can be taken away: income, a car, a house. And by the way, I dig powerboats. This is a metaphor."

He hoisted himself up onto the bar. "The other kind is *sailboat success*. I've spent some time sailing the deep oceans, so I know. If you have a sailboat, you usually have an engine so that you can motor through calms and such. If the engine breaks down or you run out of fuel, you still have the wind. No one can take the wind away from you, and even if your sails are wrecked by a storm, the wind will move your boat on the rigging alone. Sailboat success is success that can't be taken away from you, because it's built on things that, like the wind, are fundamental and eternal: peace, family, love, a passion for what you do, service to your community. Sailboat success always leads to material success, but it doesn't work the other way around. Which would you rather have?"

"So financial professionals should concentrate on family, personal passion, and community instead of selling product, managing portfolios, and allocating assets?" said the Banker.

The Guru shook his head. "Not entirely, no. Then they wouldn't be fulfilling their fiduciary duty to clients, but the nonmaterial aspects of success should be priorities. You can't work just for the financial rewards, or you'll dismiss the nonmaterial aspects of your work that are so critical. The key thing to understand is that focusing on those things will also lead to greater financial and material rewards."

"How?" the Financial Advisor asked.

"Because you're not just working with accounts, as you know, but with human beings," the Guru said. "No matter how important money is to them, people are also creatures of values, morals, and self-image. They want to see themselves as moved and motivated by nobler forces than sheer profit, and they often sincerely are. The ones who are pure product buyers might settle for a financial advisor or broker whose only attractive feature is helping them make money. The ones who want a long-term relationship want someone who is driven by values that are similar to theirs. They crave that affinity with a person who puts family ballgames before quarterly meetings and happily gives part of his commissions to important community causes. Those are the folks who build relationships that last decades, who refer new clients and stick with you when times get tough rather than shop for someone else who promises the moon."

"That does make sense," said the Stockbroker.

"But it's not just about appealing to values," continued the Guru, "that could be faked, though it would be very difficult. It's also about a personal transformation. Orienting your practice and your life on family, community, and service changes how you manage accounts, deal with products, and advise your clients." He hopped off the bar and looked around. "That's what I need!"

He trotted over to the swinging kitchen door, reached inside the kitchen, and took a wooden cutting board off a wall peg. "We're going to have a little exhibition," he said excitedly. He moved two chairs together, back to back, and placed one end of the board on each chair back so most of it hung over the floor. "You guys ever see *The Karate Kid*?"

The Banker laughed. "Are you kidding? That was one of my favorite movies growing up." The others were nodding. "My Dad used to do that wax on, wax off thing every time I washed the car. Drove me crazy."

"Good," said the Guru. "In that movie, Mr. Miyagi could have taught Daniel the karate moves he needed to know right away instead of putting him through all that car washing and fence painting. Why didn't he?"

Silence.

The Guru cracked his knuckles as he stood over the cutting board. "He did what he did because learning a martial art is not just about learning to kick and punch. It's about learning discipline and self-control. It's about personal transformation. By the time you earn your black belt and can kick the crap out of somebody, you've developed the wisdom and restraint not to. Without the journey and the struggle, you might become a better fighter but not a better person. With it, you become both, and ultimately that allows you to master the ultimate self-defense: not having to fight in the first place."

He began touching his fist to the board, then pulling it back. Touching and pulling back in a rhythm. "What you all do is like this. You can sell product and collect commissions with little to no values or passion behind what you do and make a good living, but you will be building a life around work that doesn't connect with who you aspire to be and leaves you empty because of it. Instead, you can put values and passion first and let them lead to the type of practice and clients you connect with. The experience of building that practice will transform you into a better advisor, banker, or broker and a happier, more prosperous human being—the type of person who can sustain such a practice for life. You get your black belt."

He sped up his fist pumping, inhaling deeply. It was clear what he had in mind.

"Dude, there's no way," said the Banker. "It's an inch thick."

The Guru's fist shot downward so fast it was a blur, and the board shattered down the middle while the backs of the chairs didn't move. The remaining splinters hung in the air for a second, then clattered to the floor. The other three stood stunned.

The Guru stood, breathing deeply, arm extended—then he pulled his arm back, assumed a stance and bowed. He opened his eyes. "Opened up a can of whoop-ass on it, didn't I?" he said with a grin.

The Triangle of Truth

Everyone in the room laughed, which broke the tension.

"Wow," said the Financial Advisor. "That was amazing. Could you show me how to do that?"

The Guru flashed a little slantwise smile. "What do you think I'm trying to do?" he said. Before any of them could react, he moved on. "Leave the pieces for the cleanup crew. We've got something more important on our agenda." He looked around the bar one way, then the other. "Need the right spot . . . hmm . . ."

"What's up?" asked the Banker.

"This lesson features some visuals, and I need a big enough space to do some drawing," the Guru replied. He stuck a finger in the air. "Aha!" He dashed toward the back of the bar and vanished. The other three sat quietly, wondering what was coming next.

Finally, the Stockbroker spoke up. "You guys buying any of this?" she whispered.

Both men were quiet for a few moments. "I think so," said the Financial Advisor. "This is some deep stuff. I don't think I've ever taken the time to answer the questions he's asking, but I know I've asked them myself."

"Bro, I don't think there are too many people in the financial world who aren't asking these questions. They just don't know what to do with the answers," said the Banker.

"I just know there's got to be something better than what I'm doing," the Stockbroker said, her eyes squeezed shut.

"Shh—" hissed the Banker.

The Guru bounded back into the main room, grabbed a blue marker off the bar, and beckoned toward the back of the building. "Come on, you won't want to miss this!" They got up to follow him, then stopped dead when they saw where he was headed: the door to the men's room.

"Um . . ." began the Financial Advisor.

"You want me to go in there?" asked the Stockbroker. "I don't think so. This is where I stop." She folded her arms and took a step back.

"Oh, come on," said the Financial Advisor. "You've come this far. You're not going to let the sight of a little urinal cake keep you from enlightenment, are you?"

She wheeled on him. "You know, wearing Armani does not give you the right to be obnoxious," she barked. "Besides which, your socks don't match."

The man lifted his left foot, then his right. One black, one navy.

"The lady's right," said the Guru. "You expect people to give you their money when you can't even dress yourself?"

The Financial Advisor winced and glared at his teacher, but there was a teasing twinkle in the Guru's eye, so he said, "Why the men's room?"

The Guru shrugged. "It's the biggest clear wall for drawing on, and I need the space. Shall we?" He held the door open.

The men eyed each other and shrugged, then walked into the restroom. The Guru held the door a moment longer, watching the Stockbroker, who simply shook her head. Then he shrugged and walked in after the other men, letting the door swing shut. The young woman stood alone in the dark bar, wondering what her next move was, and then heard a sound from the men's room:

"Buk-buk-buk-buk-buGAHK!"

It sounded like two male voices imitating a chicken. They repeated again and again, echoing off the tiles.

She made a disgusted noise. "That's not going to work!" she shouted to the closed door. Silence . . . and then the clucking started again, punctuated by hysterical male laughter.

She hissed, "Juveniles," gathered herself, and pushed her way through the door. She found herself in a surprisingly large and spotlessly clean bathroom with a huge vacant wall of white tiles. She stalked up to the Financial Advisor and the Banker, who were still snickering. "Just so you know, I didn't come in because of your teenage humor. I came in because I want to hear what this man has to say. Okay?"

"Sure," said the Financial Advisor, his lips still twitching.

"Buk," said the Banker quietly, and all three men broke up.

The Stockbroker looked down at her feet, then back up. "You guys are like the older brothers I'm glad I never had," she said as a smile flitted across her lips and softened her eyes.

The Guru, still laughing, wiped away tears as he said, "Children, can we get started? I didn't bring you into this lovely venue for standup night."

The Banker looked around. "You know, I've done my time in a lot of bar bathrooms, and this is the Versailles of bar bathrooms," he said. "It's huge. It's clean. I could live in here. In fact, I think I will live in here."

The Guru was walking toward the huge empty wall. "It's a perfect lecture hall," he said. "Now pay attention." He reached as high as he could and, pen squeaking, drew one side, then the next, then the next, of an enormous triangle on the pristine tiles. At the left vertex he wrote S, at the bottom point, P, and at the right point, C. Then he stood back to survey the result:

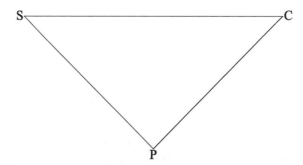

"This is the Triangle of Truth," he announced, his voice echoing. "It represents the two possible paths to the people you serve. We've been talking about becoming a different person in order to build a different practice, but this should show you clearly what that means. Let's go back to a sailing metaphor. You know what it means to sail around the Horn, right? To go around the tip of South America, Cape Horn, to get to the East Coast or West Coast of the United States?"

They all nodded.

"Good. Think of the Triangle of Truth as a map of your two options. The S stands for *sheep, shepherd, selling* and *serving.* That's your starting point, the definition of who you are and how you approach financial services. You want to get to C, which could stand for *customer* or *client, concern* or *confidence,* but to get from S to C, you need to choose which way to go. You can go the direct route, which is like going via the Panama Canal, or you can go around the Horn, which is the longer, more dangerous route down here—" He pointed to the P. "P stands for *product, performance,* and *propaganda.*"

He waited for some kind of response, but they all stood silently, watching him. "Most financial professionals choose to go around the Horn and attract business based on selling product and promising performance," he continued. "It's not about them but the product they push. That's because they believe the third P, the propaganda of the financial product providers. The goal of the product provider is to convince you that you are only as good as what you sell. According to that way of thinking, the client doesn't buy you, he or she buys a product. The lie is *you're not good enough, you are not worthy*—but if you sell more, sell my product, deliver on a performance benchmark, you can become worthy of love and approval."

He drew an arc from the S around the P to the C. "That's the long way around. When you take it, S stands for *sheep* and *selling*, because most of what you're doing is selling product to serve yourself, and you can easily end up pushing whatever other companies tell you to push. You're a sheep, and that's a problem, because your clients are sheep, and sheep don't need other sheep. They need a shepherd. And at the end of this longer journey, C stands for *customer*, because that's about all you have. You don't have relationships or loyalty. You have people who buy products and want you to be the enabler of their irrational decisions. You also have *concern*, because that's what your actions often spring from: concern that you won't make your numbers, have the respect of your peers, feel worthwhile, or like yourself."

As he apparently liked to surprise them, he abruptly slammed his palm into the wall, making them jump. "Can you make a living like this?" he boomed. "Yes, you can, but life will be hell—chasing the numbers, often putting customers into products that don't serve their needs in order to collect the commission, losing accounts to competitors, and selling out your life to chase goals that you cannot attain so that you can feel worthy—because you define yourself as nothing more than a product and performance pusher, a purveyor of a legal but addictive drug."

"Amen, brother!" The Financial Advisor's eyes bugged as he realized he'd shouted like he was at a tent revival. "Sorry."

The Guru grinned. "Don't be. Now, look at the short way around the Triangle." He drew an arc from the S directly to the C. "When you go this route, there are no products between you and the client, because the business is about you and who you are. Your value proposition is sitting behind your desk and in your chair. The truth that product providers, managers, and others don't tell you is that clients—real clients, who want real advice—buy you. Serving is the difference. When S stands for service, the client buys a shepherd, not another sheep. Let me tell you something: most financial professionals think you have to sell the best to be the best. Wrong. Selling is based on short-term thinking, and—ooh, let me write this . . ." He moved to the right of the triangle and wrote:

Short-term right is almost always long-term wrong.

The Stockbroker whistled. "That's so true."

"Remember that," said the Guru. "The best today is rarely the best tomorrow. The guy who put everything in tech stocks in 1999 was a genius until the market fell. The guy who put everything in cash in 2002 was also a genius until the market rallied the following year. Instead, your path should be a relationship based on serving, where the financial guidance you give your clients is based not on the need to make short-term numbers but on the values, character, and passions that define your life. They are based on *who you are*. This path might cost you a little money in the short term, but it will make you vastly richer over the long term and not just financially richer. This end," he tapped the C, "stands for client, because clients buy a long-term relationship with you that's based on you giving them what they need, not just what they want. If they knew what they needed, they wouldn't need you. Clients care about your values and your purpose, and they will stay with you over the long term and refer new people like themselves who will respect and value who you are, not just what you sell.

"C also stands for confidence," he continued. "The client buys your confidence more than your competence. Sheep believe that they are only as good as what they sell. The shepherd knows the truth: he or she is what the client is buying. When you are serving, you will sometimes give clients advice that makes them uncomfortable, such as taking on debt or holding in a falling market. They will listen only if you are confident, and you will only believe in your advice if you believe in what defines you. If you define yourself by what you do, you're going the long way around to success. The direct route is about who you are."

He stepped away from the wall. "This is holistic. Your industry will often define you as a seller of products and nothing more. If you let it define you, you're a fool. You!" He leveled a finger at the Financial Advisor. "What are you?"

The man stammered for a moment. "I, I, um—I'm a Registered Investment Advisor."

"True!" the Guru shot back. "But you're also a son, are you not? And a father?"

The Financial Advisor blinked. "Yes, and a brother, and a friend."

"Damn right you are." He turned to the Stockbroker, who was leaning to peer at the vending machine that dispensed condoms—an advance scout in alien territory. "See anything interesting?" the Guru snapped at her.

"Do you guys actually buy these things?" she said with a frown. "That's just gross."

"Madam!" the Guru barked, and she shot to attention. "What are you?"

"I have a Series—" she stopped, thinking. "No. I'm a sister. I'm a volunteer at a women's shelter. I'm an aunt and a marathon runner."

"That's right." He turned to the Banker. "What are you?"

"A caffeine addict and a native Californian, man," the young man said with a grin. They all laughed. "I'm also a Boy Scout, a Red Sox fan, a cousin, a boyfriend, and a surfer."

"Excellent," said the Guru. "Now you're getting it."

Faith Over Force

"Can we get the hell out of here now?" said the Stockbroker. "I feel like I'm a nun in a strip club."

In response, the Guru bowed slightly and walked to the door, opening it. The three students filed out into the bar, and as they did, the Banker said, "What's this? I didn't notice it before."

He walked over to a low, raised area in a corner of the bar that could only be a stage. On it sat an ancient upright piano, a drum kit, an electric guitar and amplifier, a microphone stand with its mic cord trailing like a serpent, and a tambourine. "Hey, this is cool. I used to play piano in a band in LA." He sat down at the piano and began to play a rippling blues riff, raining minor intervals and ending in a barrage of "bah-BAH-dah-dah-DUM" chords.

"That's pretty sweet," said the Guru. "You could also add musician to your description." He walked on stage and picked up the guitar—an aging Gibson Les Paul with peeling paint—and slung the strap over his shoulder. He flicked a switch on the amp and an accompanying toggle on the guitar, then ripped off a series of soulful riffs in a minor key, shooting a look at the Banker as he did so. The young man got the message, keying into his own series of backing chords to create a bluesy montage in 4/4 time. They came to a crescendo and then tapered off in a major key, then rested in silence.

"Nice," said the Guru.

"You know," said the Financial Advisor, "I played a little drums in high school. I could probably not make too big a fool of myself."

"The truly wise man always appears as a fool to others," the Guru said. "Go for it, sir."

The Financial Advisor took a step and then turned to the Stockbroker. "Can you sing?"

She barked a laugh. "Only in the shower, but I can play a mean tambourine."

He grinned. "Then rock on." They mounted the stage; he took a seat behind the drum kit and picked up a pair of sticks as she grabbed and jingled the tambourine. The Guru flipped a few switches on a nearby PA system and spoke into the microphone.

"Check, check." His deep, amplified voice rang out. "Cool. Ladies and gentlemen, we're going to entertain you tonight with the song stylings of Yoda and the Financiers. Let's talk about the concept of doing things right versus doing the right thing."

"What?" said the Stockbroker. "What the heck does that mean?"

The Guru turned to her. "The rhythm section is getting cheeky," he said. "In discussing the Triangle of Truth, we've discovered what you must do to build a practice based on your true worth and on relationships. I hope that by now you understand why. Now we're going to talk about how you do it." He turned to the microphone again. He strummed a 12-bar blues progression in the key of A, and the rest of the impromptu group raced to catch up. He dropped down to a one-three vamp and addressed the mic with a blues lyric clearly made up on the spot:

I woke up this mornin'
Wantin' to do things right
So I did what everyone told me
So I been workin'
Staying up all night
Selling what the other guy sold me
Yeah, I got the blues . . .
I got those sheep to the slaughter blues . . .

The Guru launched into a scorching solo as the others tried to keep up—hammering the piano keys, keeping up a rough but fairly consistent beat on the snare drum, and chiming away with the tambourine. After 16 bars, their leader came back to the mic again with another lyric:

Then I woke up this mornin'
Wanting to do the right thing
That's who I am inside
Gave my clients a warnin'
New value I would bring
Now I work with a sense of pride
Yeah, I got the blues . . .
Got them shepherd needs new sheep blues . . .

He tore into a new solo that seemed endless, rising and falling on a storm of bent notes backed by the increasingly confident rhythm of his band mates. It went on for several minutes: sweat flew from all four players, feedback crackled and purred from the amp, and the Financial Advisor broke one drumstick but kept playing with the other one. Gradually, the men noticed that the Stockbroker was dancing wildly, her eyes shut, her hair whipping around like a hippie at Woodstock, the tambourine slamming into her hip with bruising force. The other three tapered off slowly: the drums beats trickled away, then the piano went silent, and finally the Guru stopped.

The Stockbroker continued in her reverie for at least 20 seconds before she realized that no one else was playing. Sweat dripping from her hair and eyelashes, her cheeks rosy, she slowed and set the tambourine on a stool next to her. "Sorry, I was in the moment."

The three men roared with laughter, helpless and doubled over. The young woman joined them and sat on the edge of the stage, tears rolling down her cheeks. The four of them howled until their stomach muscles were sore and then tapered off to sniffling and exaggerated sighs.

"Bravo, brava," the Guru finally said, slipping down to the floor and falling into a chair.

"What exactly was the point of that? Not that it wasn't fun," said the Financial Advisor.

"Fun was the point," the Guru said. The other three came down to join him, all of them huddling at the same small cocktail table like conspirators. "Work should be fun. It should be joyful and fulfilling, like playing the tambourine. That it's not is the problem."

"And work is fun when you, what, do things right?" said the Stockbroker.

"No," said the Guru. "There's a difference between doing things right and doing the right thing. Doing things right is based on what everyone else is doing, which is usually the wrong thing. It's selling at the bottom of the market or buying at the top. It's the herd mentality at work. There are enticements to get us to go along with the herd and sanctions for not going with the herd. That's why good professional speakers rarely call on someone from the audience, because if you do, you terrify them and they start to avoid eye contact for fear they'll be singled out next. The herd offers protection, but it also often leads to selling what the others guys sell and settling for what they settle for."

There was a quiet beat. "That would have been really hard to work into a blues lyric," said the Financial Advisor.

The Guru laughed. "That's why I left it for my post-show monologue. Doing the right thing may have nothing to do with business at all. Michael Phillips said it best in *The Seven Laws of Money*: The most difficult thing for people to understand about money is that money will come to you if you're doing the right thing.[16] Notice he says *doing the right thing,* not *doing things right.* Doing the right thing is frequently one of the hardest things to do. It means acting in concert with the values and purpose that make you who you are. It may mean canceling an appointment with a top client because your family needs you.

"Let's say you're just about to implement a million-dollar financial plan, but you find out that your son broke his leg in a baseball game and is asking for you to be at the hospital," he continued. "In the moment when you cancel your appointment, you convey your values: family is more important. When you refuse to take money from a client who just wants an enabler, you're doing the right thing. You have a broad vision for how your profession should be carried out, and you live it at the office and away from the office.

"Remember when I talked about faith versus force? Force is doing things right trying to make good things happen. It's like arm-wrestling the gods and expecting to win. Faith is doing the right things and knowing that as a result, good things will always happen—in fact, good things happen the moment you choose to do the right thing. The difference is that with faith versus force, good things not only come to you but occur in multiple areas of your life."

The Stockbroker raised her hand. "So it seems that the key question for each of us is, 'What is the right thing?'"

"It is," the Guru said. "The answer is different for each of you, but you'll find it when you ask who you're serving and why. Research done by CEG Worldwide in 2001 showed that less than 15 percent of financial professionals are client-centered, defined as those who state that their highest priorities are talking to clients and building relationships.[17] The other 85 percent said the most important parts of their work were talking to their peers, analyzing the market, and strategizing. Guess who did better after 9/11? Approximately 80 percent of financial advisors didn't call their clients immediately following the attacks on 9/11. The other 20 percent more consistently weathered the stormy times, because their work was about relationships built on doing the right things *without worrying about short-term profit.*"

Perspective and Knowledge

The Banker raised his hand. "That's hard. To do the right thing is kind of a leap of faith. I know some managers who would crucify their top bankers if they left the office for anything less than the imminent death of a family member."

"I think that's what he's talking about," said the Financial Advisor. "It's a faith journey. You can't see the results right away like you can when you're just chasing the numbers. It's like crash dieting versus eating healthy food and exercising. You might see quick results with a crash diet, but it doesn't mean you're healthier. If you eat healthy foods, exercise, and take vitamins, you're going to lose weight more slowly but be healthier in the long term."

The Guru held out an arm. "Meet the master of the metaphor. Well done." The Financial Advisor bowed his head. "Doing what I'm talking about means taking the long-term view, something Americans aren't good at. Doing things right is born of a short-term, get-rich-quick perspective. Think about sheep again. They look at the ground before them: current market performance, current events, current weather. The shepherd has to have the long-term vision. He has to see the terrain ahead and the weather to come so that he can keep his sheep safe, even if it means he's uncomfortable in the short term. That is vision. The brain is linear and markets are not. Doing the right thing means training yourself to think past the linear to your big vision. "Look at it this way," he continued. "Look back at the trends of your practices over the years. How many times have you had to rebuild your book of clients because you sacrificed long-term sustainability to make a buck? Do you actually expect to create a prosperous, fulfilling, successful long-term future that way?"

There was a long lull as the other three went deep in thought. The cooling amplifier ticked.

"He's right," said the Banker. "I've had huge turnover because I've upsold business clients into products they didn't need just to satisfy benchmarks. So have almost all the other guys I work with."

"So what do we do?" the Stockbroker said. She wore the urgent look of one who sees a brief window of salvation. "I mean, how can we always do the right thing?"

"My dear, that is a question that would take months to answer," said the Guru. "Let me tell you this, and it's not something you're going to want to hear. You already know what the right thing is, each of you. You know what feels right to you, what feels rich and rewarding and human and just and empowering. That's what your work should reflect—but you often don't do it because of fear. You don't always do the right thing because at the end of the day, knowledge isn't enough. The amygdala and that dopamine rush still make you pursue short-term pleasure and avoid short-term pain at all costs. Why do you think smokers can't quit even though they know smoking annihilates their health? Yes, it's a physical addiction, but some quit. Most can't because their desire for that short-term pleasure outweighs long-term gain. Let me say it clearly, and I want you all to remember this:

Knowledge is not enough to lead to right action.

"Two factors—the drive to pursue pleasure and the sanctions for going against the norm—will prevent you from doing the right thing until you have that epiphany that we talked about," he continued. "The amygdala shuts down not only the frontal cortex but also the hippocampus, which gives us access to our long-term memory, where history and knowledge reside. Your perspective goes to hell. The shepherd must have perspective, the long view. The most valuable thing you can bring to your clients is perspective. Know history; it will tell you the right things to do. When you do them, the outcome will be in your favor and your clients' favor."

"That's the difference between the professional and the layperson in any business," said the Banker.

"Yep," said the Guru. "Let's say you're arrested for drunk driving. You spend the night in jail, and you're probably terrified, not knowing what's going to happen to you, but when you talk to an attorney, someone who knows the law and has a better perspective on what will happen, you calm down. Your irrational mind is quieted by means of the more rational ability to anticipate the future."

The Financial Advisor pointed a finger at the Guru. "But perspective isn't enough, right?"

"Correct. You can have long-term perspective and all the knowledge in the world and still not act on them," he replied. "Remember when I said that speculation was not the key to success? Well, education isn't the only key, either. The key is preparation. Since you can't make an epiphany happen, and you can't afford to wait for it, you have to prepare. You have to take steps to manage your fears—to serve instead of sell and take the long-term instead of short-term view—instead of chasing a check.

"Let's put it this way," he said, standing. "Until an epiphany changes the game, your higher values and greater vision will fight a losing battle with your amygdala and your dopamine receptors. So you've got to take proactive steps that force you to act out of a sense of service and do the right things."

"Like a smoker getting rid of every pack of cigarettes in the house," said the Stockbroker.

"Or an alcoholic pouring out all the booze in the liquor cabinet," said the Banker.

"Yes," said the Guru. "Giving yourself a safety net takes away the anxiety that you might backslide and sabotage client relationships that are newly built on a bedrock of personal values. Preparation frees you to act on faith and do the right thing in spite of yourself."

"Transformation for dummies," cracked the Banker. They all laughed.

"This is rough going," said the Financial Advisor, "but I think I'm getting what you're saying. What now?"

"I'm going to share with you how to prepare for the booby traps your brains are going to throw in your paths," the Guru said, sliding his arms into his coat. "Still working on those lists of questions? Finish them and grab your things. We're getting out of here."

Lesson Five

Knowledge without Action Is Worse Than Ignorance

"How soon 'not now' becomes 'never'."
—*Martin Luther*

"You are the embodiment of the information you choose to accept and act upon. To change your circumstances you need to change your thinking and subsequent actions."
—*Adlin Sinclair*

"People often say that motivation doesn't last. Neither does bathing—that's why we recommend it daily."
—*Zig Ziglar*

"Where are we going?" asked the Banker as the Guru led them through the bar's back door and down a dark alleyway. No sky was visible overhead; the narrow strip of open air above the tall brick buildings lining the alley was a uniform gray. It could have been 9:00 a.m. or 8:00 p.m.

"You'll see," the Guru said. He walked briskly down the dank alleyway and directly to a flight of steel stairs that passed through a building and vanished into the gloom overhead. His boots clanked on the steps as he beckoned them to go on.

The Financial Advisor looked at the others and shrugged. "In for a penny, in for a pound at this point, I suppose," he said.

The Stockbroker placed her hand on his arm. "Are you sure you want to go up there?"

The Financial Advisor nodded with a smile. "I want to find out how this all ends." He trotted up the steps. The other two exchanged a look and followed. They found themselves in a dark column of steps that curled upwards like a coil of DNA. They climbed for several minutes, gasping for breath, and then emerged into dingy gray sunlight. A concrete and steel bridge lay before them; the Guru was already walking across its span. They followed, sneaking peeks over the sides. Below lay what was unmistakably Franklin Delano Roosevelt Drive, which runs along the eastern waterfront of Manhattan. Cars crowded every inch of pavement and raced at a pace that seemed to promise imminent disaster. Once they reached the center of the bridge where the Guru stood waiting, the three stopped.

"Where are we?" said the Stockbroker, looking down in amazement. The road lay at least 200 feet below.

"There's no bridge over FDR Drive!" exclaimed the Banker.

"Apparently, you're mistaken," said the Guru calmly, "because that's clearly FDR down there, and we're looking over it from a unique vantage point for a very good reason."

The Financial Advisor shook his head. "But out there—" he pointed toward the unseen other end of the bridge, "—is only the East River. What is this bridge connected to?" He started to march toward the other end and felt the Guru's hand on his arm, gentle but firm.

"Son, I wouldn't."

The flat authority in that voice was enough. The middle-aged man eyed his companions, then came back to join them. "So, what now?" he said.

"We are here," the Guru began, "for a lesson in motivation. Think of this as the bridge to your future, if you prefer really obvious metaphors. The path to that future leads through motivation—understanding what it is and what it is not."

He spread his arms wide to indicate the busy highway below. "Behold the perfect symbol of the human brain," he said. "Chaos in motion with a million independent moving parts, all with a general direction but individual goals. The whole thing is just a lane width from breaking down into general insanity, as are we all. Each of those drivers possesses knowledge and the illusion of motivation. Do any of you know what I mean?"

They all shook their heads.

"We've talked about the fact that knowledge is insufficient to make most people change the way they do things, right?" he said.

Nods.

"Good. So far, we've made excellent progress. You've gone from learning about how your very human brains handicap you in making wise decisions, to facing the brutal truth about why you're in finance, to discovering the need to serve a purpose, to finding out that doing the right thing is the only path to that service. Now we're going to talk about why none of you will act on any of what we've discussed."

"What?" cried the Banker. "You're putting us through all this Obi-Wan stuff and you don't think it's going to make a difference? What the hell is the point?"

"Relax, son," the Guru said, putting a hand on the younger man's arm. "I didn't say that you couldn't use what I've been teaching. I said what I did to startle you and make you all realize that right now, even with what you've learned, if you walked back to your offices today, you would think about it for a few days and then go back to the way you'd been conducting business. Little if anything would change."

They fell silent; only the rush of the traffic below could be heard. "You're right," the Stockbroker said finally.

"What?" the Banker croaked.

"No, she's got it," said the Financial Advisor. He turned to the woman. "Tell him."

She cast her gaze toward the concrete floor of the bridge. "We know, intellectually, all this new information about ourselves—why we're doing what we're doing, what our purpose has been and whether it's the right one, and so on, but knowing isn't enough. Doctors know that obesity causes heart disease and diabetes, but you still see fat doctors. Police officers know how dangerous drunk driving is, but you still see cops arrested for DUI. Knowledge isn't enough, is it? We need more." She glanced up at the Guru.

He smiled. "My God, you're all learning so fast, becoming so brave." He squeezed the Banker's shoulder again. "You in particular, keep that outrage. Demand better answers. That's going to keep you from becoming complacent." He turned and waved his arm to indicate the highway below. "We are creatures of the familiar. Our brains are wired to deliver low-grade pleasure when we sink into what is familiar to us even if that something is dangerous or unhealthy. More important, we're programmed to experience a jolt of panic and fear when we encounter the unfamiliar, even if that unfamiliar thing is something to our great benefit. Human beings are uncomfortable with an amorphous sense of self—we want to be able to tell others and ourselves who and what we are in simple, clear terms. We hate ambiguity, probably because in our distant past, ambiguity about crops, weather patterns, or predators could kill us. So we cling to self-definitions: stockbroker, financial advisor, mother, smoker, veteran, reality TV addict.

"Think about what you say when someone asks you about yourself at a party: you tell them what you do to earn money," he went on. "But psychologist Martin Seligman has shown us the things that give us meaning and make us happy: engaging in satisfying work, avoiding negative events and emotions, being married, having a rich social network, gratitude, forgiveness, and optimism. Money isn't on the list, but it's the first thing we talk about. We can't even express who we are without the labels, yet not only does society not recognize the meaningful labels, it often ridicules them—so we grasp at labels defined by other people to identify who and what we are."

"I met a guy once," said the Banker after a moment of quiet, "for a business meeting in another city. I was going to pick him up, and he told me on the phone, 'I'll be the fat guy on the corner.' I didn't think anything of it until after our meeting and he started talking about how much he wanted to lose weight. I asked him, 'Then why do you call yourself *the fat guy?*' That was his self-definition, and as long as it stayed that way, he probably wasn't going to lose weight."

Volition, Motivation, and Actualization

The Guru was nodding like a bobble-head doll. "Very astute. Once we've defined ourselves in certain ways, those definitions become very comfortable and very hard to change. You all define yourselves as financial professionals who do business a certain way, who have a certain material standard of living, and who've made ethical and moral bargains that you've learned to live with, but you're not happy. You're not doing all that you should be doing for yourselves or your clients. Why? Because you've defined yourselves according to the expectations of others. If you walk away from here right now knowing that, nothing will change, for the same reason that most people don't change."

The air seemed charged with energy as he fell silent. Finally, the Financial Advisor said, "What is that reason?"

"Because change is not about what you do. It's about who you are," the Guru said flatly. "Doing comes after you've become. You have to become what you want to achieve. If you want to be thin, first you have to redefine yourself as a thin person and let your actions follow. If you want to be a financial professional who nurtures client relationships and is guided by a set of personal values rather than sales goals, you first have to become that person. When you become that person, it will be impossible for you to go back to the way you once did business. Until you be, it will be impossible for you to truly do business in a new way."

"Whoa," the Banker said.

"Indeed," replied the Guru.

"So you're saying that we need to be . . . motivated," said the Stockbroker.

The Guru grinned broadly. "Oh my, I am so glad you brought that up. You three are becoming so wise, and the beginning of wisdom is realizing all that you do not know. It leads to the ultimate lesson, which I will get to in due time, but right now, settle in and look down. We're going to have a master class in motivation."

He indicated the eight lanes of cars moving below, weaving in and out of lanes, some exiting and others entering in a stream of endless motion. "Witness the flow of humanity. There's a reason that urban planners and civil engineers call it an artery, because each highway is like a vessel and each vehicle a red blood cell on the way to wherever it's bound for."

"Making cops and state troopers the white blood cells, I guess," said the Financial Advisor. They all laughed at that one as he bumped fists with the Stockbroker and Banker in celebration of his wit.

"Just so," said the Guru, "but it's not a single organism, is it? It's a collective of individuals, each with his or her own mode of motive transport. Each one possesses two of the three fundamental forces of change. The first one is volition. Look, I'll write it out for you." He reached into his jacket and extracted a can of red spray paint. "Always come prepared."

The Banker frowned as their teacher bent to the concrete. "Dude, I didn't peg you for a graffiti artist."

"Just think of it as an environmental manifesto," he replied. He bent over and on the concrete at their feet he scribed in red paint:

Volition

He stood back up and drew their attention to FDR again. "Volition is simply the intent to move from one location to another. Each of those drivers has volition and the means to exercise it: an automobile, motorcycle, or bus pass. Volition is an unconscious force that resides at the base of the change pyramid. It doesn't take any sophistication or personal insight to engage your volition. Your brain sends signals to your foot to press down on the gas or to step off the curb. That's it. The drivers down there have volition, but it doesn't mean they have any idea where they're going. Most of them are on autopilot."

He let them think on that, turned to the concrete again, and wrote a new word:

Motivation

They peered at the new word, eyebrows rising in concert, but no one spoke as the Guru pulled their gaze back to the highway far beneath them. "Motivation is the second fundamental force, a tier above volition on the pyramid," he said. He pointed at cars exiting the parkway for points unknowable. "Look at those drivers. They are making a conscious choice to exercise volition in a direction because they want to achieve a certain goal, which could be anything from picking up their dry cleaning to meeting a date at a restaurant. Volition in pursuit of a goal is motivation."

He turned back to them as they looked out over the urban scene. "Motivation is terribly misunderstood," he said. There are many theories as to why people become motivated, but they all miss the point that motivation is not the final destination for change. That's why motivational speakers mostly talk to deaf ears. A person can be motivated by a goal, but it is usually a goal that serves his or her current state of being. That's why fear is such a strong motivator: it threatens the current state. We can also be motivated by jealousy, the desire for more money, the incentive to avoid pain or gain pleasure—the core of economic theory—and a thousand other factors, but motivation does not lead to change. Motivation isn't enough."

He stopped speaking until all three pupils turned to give him their full attention.

"You are all motivated by a desire to escape the emotional—and sometimes financial—pain of your current career path," he said, "but motivation is simply movement in the pursuit of a goal. It's doing, not being. It's the *what* without the *why*. Without the *why*, without the understanding of who you are, who you want to become, and what need is provoking the desire for change, you will take action after action but never get anywhere. That's why there's a third foundational force here that no one talks about."

He knelt once more and spray-painted:

Actualization

"That goes back to Maslow," said the Stockbroker quietly. "The hierarchy of needs."

"Yes," said the Guru. "Abraham Maslow identified self-actualization as the pinnacle of human need, the need to fulfill one's full potential for wisdom, self-knowledge, happiness, service, health, creativity, and love. Some of those folks down there," he waved his arm at the traffic, "have reached the level of actualization. They are driving to do things that are in line with their deepest values and passions, because they live in a heightened state of self-awareness. That is what is needed for true change, my friends."

The Guru stood straight, slipping the spray can back into his coat. Suddenly he seemed taller than any of them had realized. "If you want to permanently change the way you work and live, you must have meta-cognition, the self-awareness of the reason that you need to change things, and then let yourself be driven by the depth and intensity of that need. That is actualization: deep, irreversible self-knowledge that creates an irresistible need for transformation. Volition and motivation ain't gonna cut it."

"Wow." This was the Financial Advisor, who seemed a little stunned.

"Double wow," said the Stockbroker.

"I'm telling you this," the Guru said softly, "because I don't want you to waste your time. It's so easy to identify that you're unhappy and why you're unhappy and then think that because you're motivated to do things differently you're making progress. If that's where you stop, you become like most of those drivers down there: moving but not going anywhere. I don't want that to happen to you three. There's too much at stake."

The Stockbroker stepped forward, reached up to put her arms around his neck, and embraced him. When she pulled back, her eyes were moist. "Thank you."

The Guru's eyes softened. "What was that for?"

"For telling us the truth about how hard all this is going to be," she said, wiping her eyes. "For not lying to us about it being easy. It's not."

The Three Stages of Need

The Guru inclined his head momentarily. "I won't ever lie to you, children," he said. "I will tell you things you don't want to hear, but I will always tell you the truth." He began to walk back the way they had come. "Hey, our touching moment is over! Keep up; we have lots to do yet." They fell in line behind him and proceeded back down the stairs to the alley where they started only to find that the alley wasn't quite the same. Where there had been a simple corridor of dank brick, they now saw a four-way intersection.

"Was this here before?" said the Stockbroker, pulling her jacket back on.

"No, but nothing surprises me anymore," said the Financial Advisor. "I'm just going with it. I want to know how this ends."

"Amen, brother," said the Banker. He held out his elbow to the Stockbroker, who laced her own arm through his, then held her left arm out to the Financial Advisor, who linked up. Thus attached like Dorothy flanked by the Scarecrow and the Tin Man, they marched after their teacher.

The group emerged in a courtyard with a fountain at its center. It would never be mistaken for a spot in Florence or Rome: broken concrete, fountain scarred with graffiti, water dark with smelly algae, stunted trees, and cold metal benches. The sky above was blue and flawless, and they all turned their faces to the sunshine, eyes closed.

"This," began the Guru, "is our model of the dynamic of need. Actualization is a big word and sounds fancy, but at the heart of it is need. Need is the only force that provokes real change. We don't change things because we want to, but because we need to. Do you know why most New Year's resolutions are broken?"

The Banker raised his hand. "My turn to show off," he said. "Because people want to change something but don't need to do it."

"Correct. The great majority of the people who make resolutions do so for the wrong reason: external forces. They want other people to see them as thinner or to stop being lectured by their doctors because they smoke. They want to make changes for external reasons, but need doesn't come from outside you. It can only come from within you. That's one of the fallacies of motivation. It's why a woman can have 20 of her friends tell her how bad a guy is for her, but she won't do anything until she finally develops the need to change from within."

"Tell me about it," the Stockbroker said sourly.

The Banker walked into the center of the courtyard and stood on a bench. "So you're saying that we have to wait for need to hit before we can really make any changes? Seems like we're just deluding ourselves until then."

The Guru followed him into the center of the square and stood at the edge of the fountain. "No. That would be waiting for the epiphany, and as we've said, you can't count on an epiphany, but you can encourage it. Another fallacy about motivation is that it comes when it comes. That's wrong. We're not helpless." He whirled on his heel and glared at all of them. "I shared with you why people change the way they live and choose," he said. "Do you want to know *when* people change?"

The Financial Advisor said what they were all thinking. "You know, you really shouldn't ask stupid questions. Of course we do."

The Guru threw his head back and laughed. "Bravely spoken, sir! Okay, this is when people change and not before: *When their need for change becomes strong enough to overcome the brain's natural desire for the comfort of the way things are.*" They were all nodding. "In relationships, therapists often say that when the pain of staying is worse than the pain of leaving, the person will finally leave, but not before. Until the person reaches that threshold, she or he will rationalize and excuse. As entrepreneur George Shinn said, "Growth means change and change involves risk, stepping from the known to the unknown."

He picked up a stone from the concrete underfoot. "Our more primitive selves want things to stay the same as they are, even if the status quo is painful. That's why we must appeal to our higher selves in order to discover what we need to bring about change." His voice gained power. "Make no mistake— you can face the brutal truth and acknowledge the need to serve, not sell, but only when you are fully aware of the person you hunger to become will you create the need that produces a real, lasting personal revolution in the face of your natural fear of it. That is actualization. That is why knowledge is not enough."

He tossed his stone into the fountain. It disappeared in a stinky puff of algae that made them all wrinkle their noses. "Man, that thing reeks," said the Banker. "When was the last time someone cleaned it?"

"Nineteen seventy, maybe," the Guru replied. "Need! Need is the key that unlocks the door, as I think you can see. To take the step from knowledge to action, you have to cross the bridge with a big sign that reads NEED at one end. Let's talk about need. What do you three think? What's the typical human relationship to need?"

Put on the spot, each of the trio looked around at the others. Finally, the Stockbroker put her hand on the Financial Advisor's shoulder and said, "It's okay. You can speak for us."

The Financial Advisor smiled slowly and winked at her. "I'll start, anyway. We aren't good at acknowledging need." He looked at the Stockbroker as if handing off a baton.

"Most of us see it as weakness," she added, then waited for the Banker to step in.

He did. "And if we do let on that we have needs, we overdo it and become needy," he said. "We become dependent."

"Nicely done," said the Guru. "Correct. Humans have a dysfunctional relationship with need. We often have to be forced backward into acknowledging it, as with financial professionals who need to create a values-based business but focus on the numbers instead because they fear being perceived as not success oriented, whatever that means."

"I like it," said the Banker.

"There are three stages to need: feeling it, acknowledging it, and empowering it," said the Guru. "Let's talk about the first stage. You," he pointed at the Financial Advisor, "would you jump in that fountain and drink the water?"

The Financial Advisor made a face. "Not a chance."

"Quite right. It's disgusting. You have no need for it, but let's say that you've been wandering in the desert for three days with no water and you come across this fountain. You're dying of thirst. Do you drink from it?"

The Financial Advisor thought for a few seconds. "I guess I would."

"Why?"

"Because my need was strong enough?"

"Yes!" The Guru jumped up to stand on the fountain's edge, and the others stood in a curve around him. "You felt a raw need that overcame your natural revulsion. That's feeling need, Stage One."

"Sort of like needing to ride the subway to get to work in August despite the smell of armpits," said the Banker.

The Guru turned to him. "You're a funny guy," he said. "You're next. Let's say that instead of coming to this courtyard for the water, you came for the peace and quiet, to escape your stressful job. What would your colleagues at the bank say if you told them you took a mental break in a run-down fountain court?"

The Banker barked a laugh. "They'd call me a hippie slacker, I suppose."

"And you'd think the same thing, wouldn't you?"

"I guess I would."

"But then you kept coming back again and again because you got something here that you needed. What would you eventually do?"

A beat ticked by. "I guess I would eventually admit that I needed this place," The Banker said. "That's overcoming the fear of need. Reminds me of something Paulo Coelho wrote: 'You do not drown simply by plunging into water, you only drown if you stay beneath the surface.'"[18]

"Very good. That is Stage Two: acknowledging need, recognizing it, and not being ashamed of it," said the Guru. He turned to the Stockbroker. "I've already shared with you the final stage," he said. "Can you deconstruct it?"

She narrowed her eyes, then lifted her head and looked around. "I think that if I needed this place like that, after a while I would decide that it needed to be improved. I'd probably find a way to work with the neighborhood to put in a new fountain, plant trees and so on."

"Excellent! Really, really excellent!" The Guru pointed with such glee that his foot slipped, and he fell backward into the slimy water and went under. The three gasped and ran to pull him out of the fountain. Gasping and sputtering, he sat on the edge of the concrete rim and shook his head. "Damn, that reeks worse than Woodstock."

Everyone, including the Guru, dissolved into hysterical laughter. The Financial Advisor sank onto a bench, helpless. The Stockbroker leaned onto her knees, then fell over backward, which brought on even more giggles. The Banker sat heavily beside the Guru and put an arm around him. "Smooth move, man."

The Guru's laughter tapered off to chuckles. "You all got me so excited that I lost my balance and forgot myself. Yes, you've got it. We go from feeling a need, which is the basic action of fear or desire, to acknowledging the need, which is admitting that serving that need benefits us and is worthy of our attention. Finally, we empower the need to drive our action and we do something that further serves the need. Most people are at Stage One. Some people are at Stage Two but stop there. Changing your life means getting to Stage Three and *staying there*, in a constant state of self-reflection leading to action. You're never complacent."

Who Changes?

They sat in the breeze and the fading light, listening to the trickling water and soaking in all that had been said. Finally, the Guru sniffed.

"Can we go back to the bar?" he asked. "I'd like to take a shower."

This started another round of giggles, but they traipsed in a line back the way they had come: left at the surprise four-way intersection and through the beer-scented back door of the tavern. It was dark and cool and smelled like sawdust and pool chalk. The Financial Advisor's makeshift chessboard kept watch from its table.

"Will you excuse me for a few minutes?" said the Guru. "There's an employee shower in back and, well, I don't feel too fresh." They nodded and he disappeared through the double doors.

"I need a drink," said the Banker. "Anyone?"

Both raised their hands. The younger man walked behind the bar and with practiced precision, made three dry martinis, with three olives each. He handed them over to the other two, and the Financial Advisor raised his glass.

"A toast?"

"To what?" said the Stockbroker.

"The future," said the Banker.

"Which one?" said the Stockbroker. No one said anything for a few moments, and then the Guru appeared out of the back room, drying his hair. The three downed their drinks quickly.

"Man, that is so much better," the Guru said. "Everybody feeling all right?" He peered around at them.

"Refueled and ready to go, big guy," said the Banker.

"Go where?" the Guru asked.

"Wherever we're going next."

The Guru shook his head. "We're not going anywhere. We're staying right here. This is where the fun is." He set his cap back on his head; his clothing was completely dry. "What I'm getting at with all of this, kids, is that knowledge is not enough to get you to do what you need to do. You need to take action, but what drives the action is everything. If it's external motivation based on logical reasoning, you're wasting your time. If it's need based on true self-awareness of who you want to become, you're on the right path, but it's a hard path."

He went over to the bar's fireplace, piled some of the stacked wood on the grate, lit a spill of newspaper, and shoved it under the wood. After a few seconds, the wood began to smolder, then to burn. "Ah, now that is cozy," he said, rubbing his hands together. "Gather round, boys and girls. We're going to talk for a bit."

The other three pulled up chairs around the strengthening fire. The Financial Advisor yawned.

"This is nice," said the Stockbroker. "Reminds me of the fireplace at my grandfather's farmhouse."

"Settle back, because we're going to talk about the last and most important component of change," the Guru said. "We've talked about why and when, but now we're going to look at who. Who changes and who doesn't?"

They shared looks but nobody spoke up.

"Psychological studies of people who complete long, difficult courses of study versus people who quit partway through have revealed something very interesting," continued the Guru. "Who would you say is more likely to finish something long and tough, the people who research and prepare beforehand or the people who dive in and wing it?" He cocked a finger at the Banker. "What do you think, cowboy?"

"I don't know. I'd guess the people who prepared."

"Okay. The rest of you agree with him?"

The Financial Advisor and Stockbroker nodded.

"Gotcha! Good, I was worried you were getting smarter than me," the Guru said as he smiled. "No, the people who dive in and just start working finish much more often. You know why? Because they didn't overanalyze and psych themselves out with the difficulty of what they were trying to do. They just acted, and they discovered that the process itself was enough of a reward to keep going. They knew they were doing something that was making them better, smarter people, and that kept them going.

"What I'm saying is that we only truly believe something after the fact. That's human nature. We don't believe the earthquake will hit until it hits, which is why 90 percent of people don't have an emergency kit in their car. The people who prepare are those who appreciate that the value and meaning of taking action lies in taking the action, not in the result."

The Financial Advisor spoke up. "You're saying that acting is a leap of faith."

"In a way, yes," said the Guru, "but it's more. When you're acting based on actualization—and notice that both words share the same root, *act*—you're not worried about the result. The people who completed the long educational course in that psych study valued the fact of action over everything else. What mattered to them was that they were changing, not what they were changing *into*. Get it?"

"So growth should be its own reward," said the Stockbroker.

"Yes," said the Guru. He warmed his hands over the fire and added a log. "In the end, you can have actualization and awareness and need, but they must translate into action. *You must become in order to do, but then you must do in order to become.* Does that make sense?"

The Financial Advisor nodded. "Absolutely not."

The Guru sighed. "My bad," he said. "Awareness of who you want to become and the need that drives you to want to change are great, but in the end, you must change. If you don't, you'll revert back to the state you were in before the awareness came. Enlightenment has an expiration date. It can't exist in theory, only in fact. If you don't take action, it's just a mental exercise."

"And the way you take action is by taking action, desiring the process of being aware and changing, not worrying about having every step mapped out in advance," said the Stockbroker.

"Exactly!" The Guru cracked his knuckles. Silhouetted by the fire, he looked like Gandalf or another fantasy character. "What you know doesn't matter unless what you do matters. Get that one tattooed on your arm, lady and gents, but let's take this a step further.

"Let's say you're a financial advisor who's sick and stressed and miserable from years of being a slave to the numbers and selling your soul to the culture of more," he continued. "You want to run a practice that speaks to the reasons you got into the business in the first place: relationships, helping people, the thrill of changing lives. Those are your values. You feel the need, acknowledge the need, and know who you need to become, but you don't take action because it all seems too daunting. It's too much to handle. You know what I mean?"

The Stockbroker spoke through a yawn. "I do. It's this huge task, turning your life and career around. I mean, it's like managing a military campaign. There are things I would do, but each one would bring up 10 more things to do."

"I think that's what we're all facing," said the Financial Advisor. "We all want to make big changes, but we don't know where to start."

"Then don't make big changes," the Guru said softly. "Just make changes. Act. The mistake so many people make is that they think change is about waking up and everything is different. Well, once you have that epiphany, you might wake up and be different, but life is still the same. Just because you change, that doesn't mean the world changes. That takes work, but you don't have to do it all at once. You don't have to transform your life overnight. You can't, but you can begin the process and keep going—"

"Find value and satisfaction in acting rather than its result," said the Stockbroker.

"Bingo," said the Guru. He rose and walked behind the bar, grabbed a marker, and wiped his previous work off the large mirror. He went to work, eventually drawing this image:

The Continuum of Change

Results/Logic/External————————Growth/Purpose/Internal

"This is something you should also tattoo on your body. I'll let you pick the spot," he said. "What most people don't understand is that while you will never be completely fear-driven and blind to your purpose, you're never going to be completely moved by self-knowledge and purpose, either. You're always growing and changing. Nothing is static, and it's always work to stay above the fray and keep serving, aiming for our highest purpose.

"You're always going to be someplace along this continuum," he continued, running his finger along the drawing. "The point is that you are always trying to move from being moved by external motivation and the need for results toward internal actualization, greater purpose, and the desire to grow. That's why the old saw *It's the journey, not the destination* is so timeless. It's true. We don't live in a static world. Everything is always changing with time. You can never *be* anything, but man, you can sure as hell become something."

They all stopped to take that in, each thinking about what they might do to start taking action, to begin the process of change. Finally, the Financial Advisor raised his hand. "I once heard a story about Zig Ziglar. His doctor told him to lose 60 pounds, and Ziglar said, 'I can't lose 60 pounds, but I can lose two-and-a-half ounces a day for six months.' Is that sort of what you mean?"

The Guru smiled. "Yes. Change happens at the speed of life. Starting is what matters. Roger Hall, a psychologist, once said that he has a 20-40-60 plan for each day: 20 minutes of quiet, 40 minutes of reading, and 60 minutes of exercise, six days a week. That's changed his life completely. The first time he did it, did it change his life? No. The act of acting, becoming the person who would undertake that process, changed him."

"Here's a story. There's a little boy on the beach," said the Banker, "and he's throwing starfish in the water. There are thousands of starfish on the ground. A man on vacation walks out of his beach shack and sees the kid and says, "Why are you bothering? There are thousands of them! You can't save them all, so what can it matter?" The boy holds up one starfish and says, "It matters to this one.""

The Stockbroker got up, walked over to kiss the young man on the cheek, and then retreated to her seat.

He blushed, rubbed the kiss, started to stand up, then sat back down. "I have other stories," he said, which made everybody break up laughing.

"I know this isn't easy," said the Guru, coming back around to sit at the fire,
"but you're all doing really well. Let me tell you something huge." He stared into the flames for a few moments. "When you discover your needs and become the person who can fulfill them, something else happens. You become what other people need."

They all started at the revelation. The fire crackled in the silence.

"Imagine becoming what someone else needs to achieve their life's purpose," the Guru intoned quietly. "Isn't that why you got into this business in the first place?"

"Yes," said the Financial Advisor.

"Yes," said the Stockbroker, whispering, her voice intense.

"Si, señor," said the Banker.

"That's when you're truly serving. That's what it's all about."

"I thought that was the Hokey Pokey," cracked the Banker.

Laughter all around.

"You're a riot, lad," said the Guru. "Okay, you three, you're gonna love this next part. Ready to go for a ride?"

Lesson Six

If You Want to Catch a Train, Stand Next to the Tracks

"Consult not your fears but your hopes and your dreams. Think not about your frustrations but about your unfulfilled potential. Concern yourself not with what you tried and failed in but with what it is still possible for you to do."
—Pope John XXIII

"A calling is the most satisfying form of work because, as gratification, it is done for its own sake rather than for the material benefits it brings. Enjoying the resulting state of flow on the job will soon, I predict, overtake material reward as the principle reason for working."
—Dr. Martin Seligman

"Even though you are on the right track, you will get run over if you just sit there."
—Will Rogers

"A ride?" said the Banker. "What, are we walking to the subway?"

The Guru rubbed his hands in front of the fire. "That was a figure of speech. I'm going to take you on a ride all right, but we're staying here. It's quiet, it's cozy, we've got a fire and booze. Would you rather be here or a Tibetan mountaintop?"

"One vote for the pub," said the Financial Advisor, raising his hand.

"So far," the Guru began, "we've spent a lot of time taking a hard look at the mind—how fear provokes it and disconnects our reason, how we can't always believe what we think because we're driven by the need for security and pleasure, and how turning ourselves toward service and higher values can transform us. I've put you through a pretty tough boot camp of self-reflection."

The Stockbroker said, "That you have."

The Guru nodded. "I know it's been hard. It's supposed to be. If it were easy, everyone would do it, and none of you would be in the fix you're in. It's not enough. I've guided you toward facing harsh truths. I've shown you the importance of discovering the purpose you should be serving. I've shared how vital it is to find the need within yourselves to become the change that you want to see in your careers. That's all wonderful, but by itself, it changes nothing."

The Financial Advisor dragged up a low chair and sat with his back to the fire. "What do you mean?"

"Well, like I said," the Guru said, "knowledge without action is just mental solitaire. Plenty of people in this world get knowledge and get motivated to do something but never take that final step, taking constructive action. They don't even know why they don't. They just delude themselves that having the knowledge is enough and that 'one day' they'll do something with it. Then, one day, they're dead."

"Ouch," said the Banker.

The Guru stood and headed for the bar, speaking as he walked. "Do you understand why people know but don't act?"

A blanket of introspective quiet dropped over the room. The Guru ducked behind the bar; as he began mixing himself a drink, the stirrer tinkled. Finally, the Stockbroker raised her hand. "It's the amygdala again, isn't it?"

The Guru poured bitters. "Go on."

She stood. "You explained that humans make too many decisions based on our brain's natural chemistry, which drives us to seek pleasure and avoid fear. We also talked about how what we fear most is the unknown future, to the point where we'll stick with a status quo that's not working rather than pursue changes that might improve our lives but also carry risk."

The Guru was pouring something over ice. "Keep going, you're on a roll."

"Well, even after learning all these new truths about ourselves, about what we serve and why we should be doing what we do, it's not enough. We might be shocked by our own choices and feel a strong sense of regret and want things to be different, but that doesn't mean that we can overcome our innate fear of the unknown. Making things different means going into an unknown future, and we resist it even when it's best for us."

She looked around with a shy smile, realizing that she hadn't made a speech since high school debate club. The others waited a moment then broke into applause. The young woman smiled and curtsied. "I also do weddings," she said as she sat.

The Guru barked a laugh. "Funny and smart," he said. "Well said, and you said something vitally important about mindset that I don't even think you realized, but I want to touch on it." He sipped his drink, reached for his marker, and wrote something new on the bar mirror:

Wanting things to be different is not the same as wanting to change.

"Wow," said the Financial Advisor.

"That," said the Guru as he whacked the mirror glass with the flat of his hand, "is the footbridge over the canyon that separates the people who gain knowledge and feel motivation but don't ever do anything and those who make that leap and truly change their futures."

"Wanting things to be different is passive," said the Stockbroker.

"But wanting to change means taking action," said the Banker. "You can want something to happen without actually doing anything to make it happen. That's easy. I had a buddy who talked for three years about leaving his cheating girlfriend. Drove us crazy, but he never did anything. She finally left him."

The Guru walked back around the bar and sat among the other three again, drink in hand. The flickering firelight aged his face and brought out its clefts and shadows. "You've all got it. It's a leap across a chasm from desire to action, and not everyone can make it. Wanting things to be different is like being buried alive—you know things are not right and you know the steps you should take to change them, but you cannot take action. Your amygdala won't let you. So instead, you bargain with your mind. You tell yourself one or all of the three great lies: having the knowledge means you've already changed, you will make the changes sometime in the future, or some sign will tell you when it's right to step into that unknown future—and you do nothing." He took a sip, then sighed.

"It's sad," said the Financial Advisor. "You just described so many people I know. They know what to do but can't do it. They complain about their weight but seem powerless to take the action to change it."

"Right!" said the Guru. "That's the difference between wanting things to be different and wanting to change. Action. We wait for the wrong reasons. We wait, assuming that one day, a switch will flip and we'll have the will power or entrepreneurial drive we didn't have the day before, and that's nonsense. We don't just become different. We have to make ourselves different by becoming actualized and then taking action. Love is something that you do."

"This is what people don't understand," he continued. "We make transformative decisions based on emotion, not on intellect. So you can't just *decide* to change; you have to feel that you have no choice. That's the epiphany that rewires your amygdala so that the pain of staying the way things are becomes greater than the potential pain of changing and facing the unknown. That emotional epiphany redirects your life and career path, and it can't be forced. You can't say, 'Today, I'm going to have an epiphany, and everything's going to be different.'"

More Important Than Fear

They absorbed this briefly, and the Stockbroker said, "So we're screwed."

The Guru blinked and stopped in mid-drink. The Banker, who had placed his feet on a table, brought them to the floor with a crash. The Financial Advisor stared silently.

"I'm not trying to be flippant, just keeping it real," she said. "You've already said that it's impossible to force an epiphany, and if that's the only thing that brings on change, there's no way to do it. We just do what you said before, talk about it, make a few changes, and after a few weeks, go back to the way things were."

The Guru smiled at her. "You have a knack for cutting right to the marrow of things, do you know that?" he said. "You don't tolerate any BS. You're also driving right by the nuance of things. Slow down that keen mind and smile, and I'll tell you why there's hope."

The Stockbroker stared at the Guru for a few seconds, then slowly rose from her seat, walked to him, and sat on the thick, old Persian rug at his feet. A beat later, the Financial Advisor followed, then the Banker—one on each side of her. They looked up at their teacher like supplicants approaching the Oracle of Delphi.

The Guru slowly inclined his head to recognize the gesture of respect, then addressed his class. "Ambrose Redmoon wrote, 'Courage is not the absence of fear, but the belief that there is something more important than fear.'[19] That's what drives the process of personal change. Notice the word belief. This is an act of faith. Faith is the opposite of fear. When you feel that something is important enough, despite the fear that it makes you feel, you'll do it. Let's say you have to walk across a balance beam between buildings 50 stories high. The beam is 200 feet across and the conditions are windy. Would you walk across for 10 dollars? Hell no. Would you walk across for 100 dollars? No. Would you do it for a million, ten million, or a hundred million? No, no, and no. What if someone was about to drop your child on the other side? You would walk across it for nothing. Your love is stronger than your fear!"

He stood up and began pacing around the room, getting into a rhythm. "I'm not talking about that miraculous epiphany," he continued. "Taking action after the universe gives you a sudden kick in the teeth is easy. Look how motivated religious converts are or political acolytes. They'll sell everything they own and go to the ends of the earth, but that's because they've already had their epiphany. There's another truth about epiphanies: they're not always rational. You can have an epiphany that tells you to leave your spouse, abandon your kids, and join a cult, but that wouldn't exactly be taking your life in a positive direction."

The Financial Advisor raised his hand. "So you're saying that there's a middle ground between accepting potential lies and waiting for the epiphany that might never come?"

"Bingo," said the Guru. "There is a third way, a middle way. If you've spent 15 years working as a financial professional serving yourself and the numbers, worrying more about consistent sales growth than whether you love what you do and feeling empty and cold because of it, you have the fuel it takes to find the third way. You need to have something stronger than fear to take on the hard work, because change without an epiphany is bloody hard work. You don't have an evangelical vision. You don't feel inspired. You mostly feel so repelled by the way your life is today that you're willing to do what terrifies you based only on faith that somehow, the future will be better if you do."

"The stock market is the same way," he continued. "Staying in the market when it's down, which is the advice most people give their clients, is based on the faith that things will be as they were in the past, right? For that advice to work, we need to have faith that the cycles of the past will repeat themselves. It's the dynamic we've already talked about: tomorrow will be brighter if we continue to do what is right and have faith that it will produce a better result. You need some things to be in place before you'll have that kind of faith in your career and take yourself out of the territory of comfortable lies and beyond your fear."

"What things?" asked the Banker.

"Passion and a sense of mission," said the Guru with an avid gleam in his eyes. "Do any of you know your professional mission statement? Not your company's but your own? When was the last time you read it? Does it still make sense after what you've learned today? If it doesn't, what should it say?"

They were silent.

"I thought as much. Not to worry, that's normal," he continued. "What is your mission? You must know that, because your mission will feed your passion. The word passion is incredibly overused, but do any of you know what it actually means?" Silence. "Suffering! Passion means suffering, as in 'the passion of Christ.' Something you are passionate about is something for which you will suffer. When you transform your career, your life, and yourself into something that defies conventional wisdom, you guarantee that you will receive sanction from others. You are exercising your passion, doing something that you know will cause you suffering and doing it anyway.

"Passion is stronger than fear," he went on. "What creature in nature takes action to cause its own suffering? Only us! Our minds give us the freedom to choose to evolve. We can choose to suffer because we have faith that at the end of that suffering lies a better life, a better us. When an entrepreneur starts a company, she knows she's going to face years of barely scraping by and good odds that she'll lose it all, but she does it eagerly. Her passion outweighs her fear, and she's willing to suffer. A man trying to get in shape at age 50 knows that he's going to work and sweat and give up favorite foods and suffer setbacks but does it anyway. His passion for looking better and being healthy is more important than his fear of failure. In fact, we suffer knowing that the process of suffering makes us stronger and wiser. Again, doing the right thing becomes its own reward."

"So we're supposed to suffer?" said the Banker. "I gotta tell you, man, that's a sales pitch you need to work on."

The Guru laughed. "You're not supposed to suffer," he replied. "You can choose not to, but you will guarantee that nothing will change. If you step into the kind of wholesale change we're talking about, you will suffer without question. One reason is attachment. Attachment is the key to suffering. What are you all attached to? Your sales ranking? Your title? Your income, certainly. Approval from your peers and superiors? We become attached and the more attached we are, the more we make bargains with ourselves to justify keeping what we're attached to. 'Next year, I'll start working with clients who fit my values.'"

"Next month, I'll take time off for a vacation," said the Financial Advisor.

"In three years, I'll go back to school and do what I really want to do," said the Stockbroker.

"Right!" said the Guru. "Why not today? Because today demands action, and action is scary, so we bargain and we lie and we grow comfortable with both. That's why suffering is a blessing. When you're suffering enough in your career or your relationship, it flags errors in your thinking. Suffering is your personal lie detector. You can either continue to rationalize—to tell yourself what speaker Bob Burg calls rational lies—or you can accept your passion, face your fear and take action."

"So we should be doing what makes us suffer," said the Banker.

"Precisely. Ask yourself what would take the most courage for you to do in your career, what would cause you the most anxiety, fear, and embarrassment in the eyes of others. Then do that thing. That's the short road to humility and a better life. We suffer because of how we think, and we suffer more when we face that thinking, because we realize that where we are is a product of who we have let ourselves become. That realization hurts, but only by facing it and then leaving it behind can we become someone else. Giving and serving others will change you, make no mistake. It will make you fearless in the realm of who you are and what you do. That's pure freedom."

The Guru had climbed back onto the small stage and sat down at the piano. The others circled around the small wall that surrounded the fireplace seating and sat in chairs facing the stage. The Guru began lightly playing.

The Elephant Keeper

"I know exactly what you're talking about," said the Financial Advisor. "I have a longtime friend—and it really is a friend, not an allegory for me—who has lived in New Jersey his whole life. He hates his career there, hates the politics, hates the lack of opportunity, hates it all. He talks all the time about getting out but never does anything. He was offered a job a year ago by a company in California that would have been perfect for him, and when he was considering it, he said to me, 'If I don't leave Jersey now, I may never leave!' He turned the job down, and he's still there. I didn't understand why until now."

"Now you understand that your buddy feared being pulled into his destiny more than he feared staying where he was miserable," said the Guru. "That's what happens when you don't have the passion that makes suffering bearable. We don't really want disruptive change to enter our lives; we want things to stay neat and predictable. Destiny coming to call means we're going to have to do things differently and enter the unknown of our own free will. That's terrifying. Your pal would rather rot, sticking with the sure thing in New Jersey, than make a bet on a potential better life in California, because he fears change. A shame."

The Financial Advisor nodded as the Guru played a blues riff in B on the keys. "I think he," he began, working on a thought that clearly was morphing even as he spoke, "has bound himself in rules that he's given other people the power to enforce, like his boss. Because he can't or won't defy those rules, he's trapped."

"Yes!" This was the Stockbroker, her eyes alight. "I do the same thing. I think we all do. We all tag ourselves with self-imposed obligations and rules on how we're supposed to live and work and worship and think. Then we're afraid to break them. It's like locking yourself in handcuffs, giving someone else the key, and then refusing to ask that person to unlock you."

"Brilliant, both of you," the Guru said. He played a bit of Händel's "Hallelujah Chorus" in celebration. "Yes, we wind ourselves in rules like shrouds and let others do the same. After a while, the cords that bind us become safe. It's like what the character in the film *The Shawshank Redemption* said about prison walls. You hate them, then you get used to them, and when enough time goes by, you depend on them. What formerly kept you imprisoned now protects you. Have the walls changed? No. You have changed. You have become ruled by fear.

"Let me tell you a story," he continued. "In India, they train elephants to be submissive to a keeper by chaining them to a stake in the ground when they are babies. The baby elephant pulls and pulls against the stake but goes nowhere. Eventually, he becomes conditioned that the rule of his life is that he cannot move without permission. By the time the elephant is a three-ton adult, a keeper can restrain it with a small rope. How is this possible? The elephant is a hundred times stronger than the keeper; he could rip the keeper's arms off with zero effort, but the rule has been established in the elephant's mind: when the slightest pressure on the rope comes, you stop. This is his lot in life."

"Are you saying that we're stuck where we are now because of the rules we made for ourselves," said the Banker.

"Partially," replied the Guru, "but also because you have let others make rules that define you. You're surrounded by rules, definitions, and self-imposed obligations. I must make X per year, I must have Y rank in my company, I must have Z number of clients in my book, and so on. Others also make rules that have equal power: what is acceptable in your company culture, who is rewarded and who isn't, and so on. You're allowing others to define your value and giving your power away. Most people think the Biblical story of the prodigal son is about the son who left and blew all the money and then came back. It is, partially, but it's also about the son who stayed and obeyed the rules and became self-righteous about it. People sit in church and think, 'I obey, so I'm worthy!' They think they're avoiding Hell by following rules and they don't see that they're already in Hell—thinking that they can perform their way into Heaven.

"When you see a guy receiving his salesman of the year award on stage and he's crying, he's saying, 'I'm finally worth attention and love,'" the Guru continued. "When you have that kind of lie in your mind, you're in prison. You'll jump through whatever hoops someone puts in front of you so that you can stay within their rules and keep getting a reward. You're a trained sea lion doing tricks, or turning tricks, for a herring. You're not just your job. You're also a parent, a child, a spouse, a sibling, a friend. Why aren't those definitions just as important as the definitions attached to money and career? Because you're not making them important. You're letting others define your value and make the rules, and they will do so in ways that leverage you to their advantage."

"To live is to war with trolls," the Banker said.

"What?" said the Stockbroker.

"Henrik Ibsen wrote that," the younger man said. "To live is to war with trolls."

"Yes. What do you think he meant?" asked the Guru.

The Banker scrunched up his face. "I think," he said after a moment, "that he meant there are always people who will try to stifle your passion and vision with their small mindedness and fear so that you don't become someone they perceive as greater than they are, because then they can't exploit you."

"Very good."

"But," said the Financial Advisor, "I think he was also talking about something else. The trolls are also us, our fears, living under the bridge and trying to keep us from crossing, just like you were talking about. The bridge between the way things are and the way they can be. Ibsen thought suffering and struggle were great blessings, even if you didn't ultimately succeed. Life is a war, and it means loving the struggle."

In response, the Guru threw down a red-hot jazz riff straight from Thelonious Monk, drawing grins from the three students. He finished with a dazzling flourish and said, "Yes! Brilliant! You've got to find that perspective that it's staying static that's fearful, not change. When you do, you'll throw off the rules and redefine yourself. Imagine a woman runner going up a hill in a race. She's getting angry because she keeps expecting the course to level off at some point and it isn't. Her expectations for her experience aren't being met. Then something clicks and she says, 'Wait, this entire race is uphill!" She changes her mindset, sheds her limits, and takes off."

Creating Inevitabilities

The Stockbroker piped up as she crossed her arms. "So you change your internal rules, and you get a fresh perspective that lets you fear change less than you fear staying the same. That still doesn't get us all the way across the bridge. There's still what cable companies call 'the last mile.' Action. I don't want to wait 10 years for my epiphany to strike. That makes all my new perspective and self-definition sort of useless, don't you think?"

"Absolutely," the Guru said, playing a brief classical interlude. "You're right not to wait, because if an epiphany is anything, it's unpredictable. There are two conditions under which an epiphany strikes. The first is in the infliction of existential terror. Do any of you know what I mean?"

They looked at each other, and finally the Financial Advisor lifted a finger. "A heart attack might be an example," he said.

More blues, segueing into rockabilly and Fats Domino at the piano. "Yes," the Guru said. "A man eats saturated fats, gets obese, and doesn't watch his blood pressure, and then when he's 57, bam! He has a coronary. He's rushed to the ER, he has a balloon angioplasty or even a bypass, and vows to lose 50 pounds and get in shape. He never had an interest in exercise before because he engaged in that most pernicious of self-delusions: It won't happen to me. Most of us tell ourselves that lie. Our house won't be the one to burn down, our job won't be eliminated, we won't be the ones to have our identity stolen, we can smoke for 40 years and not get lung cancer, and the big one, we won't die. Does anybody really, deep down, accept that one day they're going to die? I think the *memento mori*, the reminder of death, is the greatest blessing on earth because it reminds us to cherish and use every day."

He played a vague jazz tune as his audience sat, rapt.

"When that delusion is shattered by events, an epiphany often follows," he went on. "The guy who had a heart attack becomes a fitness freak. The woman whose home comes within 20 yards of burning in a wildfire finally gets fire insurance. The guy who gets laid off goes back to school for his master's. Who wants to wait for that kind of awful experience? For one thing, you might not survive. Fifty percent of heart attacks are fatal. How sick with fear do you have to be to wait for disaster before you'll take action that you know is good for you?"

"If the careers of some of the advisors I know are any indication, pretty sick," said the Financial Advisor. "I think the majority of people in my profession are unhappy or downright miserable and know it, but they can't seem to get free of that vortex. It's because they're waiting for something to change instead of making it change, right?"

A boogie-woogie piano beat this time. "Right," the Guru said. "Let's pose a question to the class. Ma'am, can you puzzle out what the other path of an epiphany is?"

The Stockbroker smiled, and then furrowed her brow and dropped her chin into her hands. The Guru began to play the theme from the TV show *Jeopardy*, and she shot him a look with a slim smile. Finally she said, "The only thing I can think of is seeing results. When you see results, sometimes you get the ache to see more, and that keeps you going." She looked at the Banker, seated next to her, for confirmation. He gave her a thumbs-up.

"That's right. I'm proud of you," the Guru said, his tone warm. "That's exactly it."

"But how do you get results when you can't take action because of fear? That's a catch-22," the Banker said.

"Sir, you have just won *Jeopardy*," said the Guru, playing the theme again. "You'll get a home version of our game and a bit of knowledge that will change your life. That is the trick, isn't it? How do you act and see results when you can't act because you haven't had your epiphany? The answer is that you unplug from the epiphany. You don't wait for it to come. You disconnect from the need for a sensation that is stronger than your fear. Instead, you go back to an earlier lesson: *you do the right thing,* and you have faith that doing so will produce the outcome you desire."

"You have to 'hack the epiphany' by putting yourself in the position where you have the best possible odds of having a transforming experience," he continued. "You have to trust that if you take action, despite it being outside your comfort zone, and set up systems that give you no choice but to do things differently, you will produce results that will eventually bring you that epiphany. Basically, you're putting yourself in the neighborhood of the epiphany and waiting for it to find you."

"If you want to get on the train, you'd better stand next to the tracks," said the Banker.

"Yes," replied the Guru. "For example, take this piano." He played an intricate classical flourish. "I play, but if you don't, and I want you to take an interest, I put you in a room with a piano. Eventually, if you're around the instrument long enough, you're going to at least try to play it, even if that just means "Chopsticks." When you want a result, the one essential thing you must do is put mind and body in a place where that result is one easy step away. You can't play the piano if you're not near one. You can't change your financial practice if you don't start changing it."

He then swept into a rendition of "A Night in Tunisia" that got the three snapping their fingers until the Banker and the Stockbroker stood up and started dancing together with practiced steps while the Financial Advisor watched and smiled. When the song ended, they applauded.

"You play beautifully," the Financial Advisor said.

"I should. I've had a long time to learn," replied the Guru. "That's the epiphany for the would-be pianist: 'I can actually play!' When you get the result you've sought for so long, suddenly you hunger for more, and you'll make whatever changes you must to keep enjoying that success. For a financial professional, the equivalent of locking yourself in a room with a piano is imposing systems on yourself that give you no choice but to do things differently. I call that creating inevitabilities."

"Can you be more specific?" said the Stockbroker. She was perspiring from the dancing but looked very happy.

"Of course I can, but I'd rather not. How about you three specify for me? What could you do in your practice tomorrow that would force changes on you even though you still feared making wholesale changes?"

They all dropped deep into thought—finally, the Financial Advisor raised his hand. "I could cut loose the third of my clients that I don't enjoy working with," he said.

"That would certainly force change," the Guru said. "I like it. What else?"

"I could sign up for personal training sessions that started every day at 5:30, so I'd have an excuse to leave work on time for once and stop working until the late night talk shows come on," the Banker said.

"Good," said the Guru. "More?"

The Stockbroker laughed sharply. "I could give my notice, collect my accrued vacation pay, and walk out the door into unemployment," she said. "How's that for forced change?"

"It's an option and not always a bad one," the Guru said. "You're all on the right track. What you want to do is to take action that doesn't let you backpedal and has high odds of producing positive results in your practice. When those results come, you're more likely to say, 'Wow, I can do this, it really works!" If the results are in line with your passion and purpose, you've got your epiphany. You'll do anything now to keep working in that place of passion and purpose. You become an unstoppable force.

"For instance, your idea about cutting clients," he continued, pointing to the Financial Advisor. "I like it. It's realistic and strategic. Why work with people you don't enjoy? You do it, you cut them loose, refer them out. Suddenly, you have more time for the clients you enjoy. You do better work for them and enjoy it more. You get better results. They refer new clients who are like them. In a year, you're likely to be back to the majority of your former book size and of your old income. You'll get more money per hour and more joy per client. You realize, 'Hey, it worked!' The scales drop from your eyes, and you see all the other steps you could take to earn more in less time and with more delight and fulfillment. How cool is that?"

"So standing next to the tracks is about taking decisive action while your amygdala is saying, 'No! Don't do that!'" said the Banker.

"Yep," said the Guru. "That is the only way to make changes without the hitting bottom kind of epiphany. Look at it this way. You are here for a reason, each of you. You are being pulled toward your destiny from one side and resisting it on the other. That tension is why you're miserable. If you wait for the right time to act, it's like trying to reach the speed of light: you can never quite get there. The conditions are never going to be perfect to force yourself into fear; you just have to do it. We spend our lives in a comfort zone when we should be finding our discomfort zone. Now is decision time for all of you. If you want to make real changes, you have to give yourselves no option to turn back."

"Crossing the Rubicon," said the Financial Advisor. "The point of no return."

"Cortez burning his ships upon reaching the New World," said the Stockbroker.

"Ben Affleck making *Gigli*," said the Banker. The other three stared at him, eyebrows raised. He grinned. "Man, there was no going back after that."

Everyone laughed.

"All of you are right, even Mr. Funnyman," the Guru said. "You've got to reach that mythical point where you can only go forward, because your fear will try to get you to retreat. Understand this: fear will keep you where you are until you can find a belief that is more important than your fear. The self-created epiphany that you can lose weight, or save money, or work from a place of passion instead of profit and still make a great profit—that's your belief, but it won't come to you. You have to go get it. We're past knowledge now. It's all about action."

He climbed down from the stage and pulled a table and four chairs around it into a circle. After sitting down, he pulled a battered deck of playing cards from his jacket, beckoned the others to sit down around the table, and began shuffling the cards with expert dexterity.

"What's this?" asked the Financial Advisor.

"Time for the final lesson," the Guru said. "Keep your head and arms inside until the night has come to a complete stop. We're going to play a little game." He began dealing.

Lesson Seven

Strap Yourself to the Mast

> *"Whoever undertakes to set himself up as a judge of Truth and Knowledge is shipwrecked by the laughter of the gods."*
> —*Albert Einstein*

> *"Humility is the foundation of all the other virtues. Hence, in the soul in which this virtue does not exist there cannot be any other virtue except in mere appearance."*
> —*Saint Augustine*

> *"Pride slays thanksgiving, but a humble mind is the soil out of which thanks naturally grow."*
> —*Henry Ward Beecher*

The Guru began expertly dealing cards, two to a person, face down. Then he stopped. "Wait a second," he said. "What are we going to use as chips?"

They all looked around and finally the Financial Advisor said, "Coasters."

"That's it," said the Guru.

The Financial Advisor rose, collected a large stack of coasters, and brought them back to the table like a waiter balancing a stack of dishes. He measured off 10 coasters, creating four approximately even stacks, and handed a stack to each of the other players.

"I suppose we can trust your counting abilities," cracked the Stockbroker.

"I should hope so," replied the Financial Advisor. "Now, what's the game?"

The Guru shuffled his coasters in his right hand like an expert gambler with casino chips. "Texas Hold 'Em," he said with a sly smile, "the classic poker player's form of poker. You all know the rules?" He peered around the table.

The two men nodded, but the Stockbroker frowned.

"No problem," said the Guru. "Each player gets two hole cards face down. Then I deal three community cards face up, called the flop. Each of us plays those cards along with the ones in our hands. We bet before the flop, then after the three cards are dealt. Then I deal a fourth card, called the turn, and we bet again. I then deal a final card, called the river, and we bet a final time. Whoever is still in the game uses the cards in their hand and the cards on the table to make the best five-card hand. Clear?"

The Stockbroker furrowed her brows. "As mud," she grumbled. She looked up at the men. "Don't worry, I'll get it. I'll own you boys by the end of the night."

"The secret to Hold 'Em," said the Banker as he eyed his hole cards, "is knowing mathematical probability, what your odds are of beating your opponent's likely hand."

At that, the Guru cracked his knuckles like gunshots. "That's one secret," he said. "There's another. It's why we're playing this game. This is where we wrap up all that I've taught you under a single word."

"What word?" said the Financial Advisor.

The Guru eyed him evenly. "Let the games begin," he said. He threw a coaster into the center of the table as a bet. The others followed his lead. He tucked one card from the deck beneath his glass, spun three onto the table, and turned them over: a nine of diamonds, a queen of spades, and an ace of diamonds.

"In researching for his book *Good to Great,* Jim Collins learned something truly fascinating about great companies," the Guru said. "When he met with the leaders of the companies, he was surprised at what he found. He called them Level Five Executives and defined that person as someone who has extreme personal humility combined with intense professional will. Do you know anyone who is both humble and has an intense professional will? They are hard to come by. Where you find intense professional will, you usually find an ego to match."

The Banker grinned. "Ain't that the truth," he said. "That describes the CEO of every bank I've ever worked for."

"I bet two." The Financial Advisor threw in two coasters.

The Stockbroker looked hesitant, then followed suit. "Two," she said.

"Sir?" the Guru said to the Banker.

The young man tossed in two oversized chips of his own. As he flipped another card into the community pile—a six of hearts—the Guru continued. "Collins describes what he calls the window/mirror dynamic. Most people, when things go well, they look in the mirror and look for evidence that they are the cause of the good. When things go bad, they look through the window to find other people or outside circumstances to blame. But Level Five Executives do just the opposite. When things go well, they look out the window and give credit to their people. When things go poorly, they look in the mirror and ask, 'What can I do better?' They have the humility to admit that they do not have all the answers. That doesn't diminish their ego, because their worth goes beyond their performance at the office."

He knocked on the table with his knuckles. "Check."

"That means you pass on betting," the Financial Advisor said to the Stockbroker, who smiled and nodded. He knocked to indicate a check, and the Stockbroker and Banker did the same. The Guru tucked one more card under his glass and then flipped the river card face up onto the table. A jack of diamonds.

"Nice card," said the Banker. "Possible flush draw."

"Humility," said the Guru, "is the final brick in the new career path you're all trying to build. You need humility in order to be willing to make the kinds of changes that you must make if you're going to send your future in a new direction. Without humility, you won't overcome the natural limitations of your human brain. According to Daniel Pink, the author of *A Whole New Mind*, the left and right brain are not as independent as we've thought. We need both to be whole, but I say that we have discounted the part of the brain responsible for empathy, intuition, and inspiration, to the detriment of the financial industry. You and yours have become all about the numbers: mathematics but no poetry. Einstein but no Shakespeare. That means you're only doing half your job with half of your selves. You're on a heroic journey, you know."

He slapped down five coasters in the center of the table. "Five."

The Financial Advisor whistled and threw in his cards. "Too rich for me," he said.

The Stockbroker was next. "Should I bet?" she asked the Financial Advisor. She peered intently at the Guru, trying to uncover something revealing.

"He's betting like he has a strong hand," replied the Financial Advisor, "but he could also be bluffing. You have to calculate the odds of both based on what you know about your opponent."

She chuckled. "I know I don't want to bet against this opponent." She mucked her cards.

The Banker eyed the Guru aggressively, hesitated, and then threw in seven coasters. "Raise two," he said with a gunfighter's bravado.

The other two raised their eyebrows, but the Guru was inscrutable. "Now we've got us a game," he said. "Let me tell you a little story about humility while I'm deciding whether I should call your raise. Ulysses in *The Odyssey* was the only one of the great mariners of his age to survive sailing past the island of the Sirens. They would sing songs that seduced men into running their ships aground on the rocks and killing the whole crew, but when it came time for Ulysses to sail past the Sirens, he did not rely on his knowledge of the Sirens' power to save him. He was humble enough to say, 'I'm just a man. I need to take steps and prepare,' and he stuffed wax in the ears of all his crewmen. Someone had to be able to hear the wind and waves, and as the captain, that meant Ulysses could not put wax in his ears. So what did he tell his crew?"

The other three sat silent, hypnotized by the story.

"'Strap me to the mast,' he told them," the Guru continued. "So his crew bound him to the mast, and when they sailed past the Sirens, Ulysses could head their song and wanted to follow it to his death but could not. He and his crew survived. Why? Because he was humble enough to know that his knowledge did not make him immune to his weaknesses as a man. He was humble enough to acknowledge those weaknesses and take steps to overcome them through preparation. His humility made him wise—he did not think himself stronger than the forces that would have destroyed him." The Guru considered for a moment and then pushed in his remaining coasters. "All in."

"That means he's bet everything, and our friend has to bet it all as well or fold," whispered the Financial Advisor to the Stockbroker.

"I feel a hard lesson coming on," she whispered back. The Financial Advisor nodded.

The Banker glared at his opponent, hesitated, looked at his hole cards, looked at them again, and pushed in all his coasters.

"Call," he said confidently. "Show me."

With a sliver of a smile, the Guru flipped over his cards: a ten and king of diamonds.

"Nut flush," he said.

"That means he has the best possible flush," said the Financial Advisor. "It's an unbeatable hand right now."

The Banker grinned, shrugged, and tossed down his cards. "You've cornered the market on Corona cardboard, man," he said.

The Guru reached over and flipped up the Banker's cards: a nine and a six. "You called my all in with two pair and a flush on the board?" he said. "Why?"

The Banker shrugged. "I thought you were bluffing."

The Guru gathered the cards and began shuffling, shaking his head. "No," he said, "that's not why. You lost because you had no humility. You couldn't accept the idea that I might know something you didn't or be in a stronger position. You had to win at all costs. That's the cell so many people in the financial world are locked in. They've bet their entire sense of self-worth on what they earn instead of who they are and what they stand for. When you do that, you can't afford to lose or in your own eyes you become worth less and therefore worthless. You convince yourself that you know all and can handle anything, and you get sucked in or suckered, like I suckered you."

The Tyranny of Certainty

The Guru shuffled the cards now not like a Vegas dealer but like a magician, arcing them from hand to hand at least three feet across, the sound like a flock of pigeons startling into the air. He began dealing another hand. "I'll spot you some chips," he said to the Banker, sliding some coasters toward him, "but you owe me a beer."

As he dealt, his voice deepened. "I'm going to kick you all out of here after this lesson. You're ready. You've learned almost everything I have to teach you about transforming your careers and your lives, but there's one more important thing I have to pass along, and that's this: cherish and celebrate what you don't know." He dealt two cards, face down, for each of them.

"What we don't know?" said the Stockbroker. "It's what we don't know that can bring us down, end our careers, even land us in prison. How can we celebrate that?" She picked up her cards, looked at them with no expression, and set them down.

The Financial Advisor picked his up and winced.

"Poker face," jabbed the Banker.

"Man, the last time I saw a pair this ugly was when my sister brought her twins to the house," the Financial Advisor said. "Those are some homely kids." He flipped his cards away. "Fold."

The Guru checked his cards impassively. "You rely on knowledge, don't you, ma'am?" he said. "Three." He tossed a trio of coasters into the center. "You figure being a woman in a profession dominated by men means you have to be better than everybody just to break even. You have to know more and be tougher than everyone else, right?"

The Stockbroker froze, staring back at him. Finally, she said, her voice almost a whisper, "I used to think that." She called his bet. The Banker was in as well.

The Guru grinned. "Those are the most hopeful words this side of 'I don't know,'" he said. He dealt the three community cards: king of hearts, king of clubs, and three of spades. "We demand perfection from ourselves and that means knowing everything, but knowing everything in a financial services profession, in a world that is inherently impossible to predict, means we're setting ourselves up for failure at every step. We insulate ourselves by clinging to what we think we know. It becomes our religion. Let me tell you, nothing holds a person in prison like the tyranny of false certainty."

The Stockbroker threw two chips into the center. "Your bet," she said to the Banker. He winked and folded.

The Guru called her bet and flipped over the turn card, a seven of clubs. "Let me ask you all this: why does Alcoholics Anonymous work? There are no hard and fast success rates out there, but let's say that 10 percent of the people who attend AA quit drinking for life. That's much higher than if they tried to stop on their own. Why? What is it about the ones who succeed?"

The Stockbroker threw in her last three coasters. "All in," she said and then paused, "all in. It's because they go all in, isn't it? They have nothing left, no choice but to change or go to prison."

The Guru called her bet. "Last card," he said, sliding one card under his glass. "That's part of it but not all." He flipped the last card up: a jack of diamonds. "But I like your all-in reference. Yes, they surrender completely and humble themselves. They admit they are helpless. They also admit that knowing that their alcoholism will kill them does not have the power to stop them from drinking. They have the humility to admit they don't know what to do and don't know what lies ahead, so they open themselves to whatever helps them take control. Their ignorance becomes power. When you set aside certainty that has gotten you into a corner and celebrate what you don't know, you open the door to discovering new knowledge that leads you somewhere new. You overthrow the tyranny of certainty."

He flipped over his cards. "Three sevens."

She threw hers on the table. "I think that's a full house, right?" Indeed it was, kings full of threes. She'd gotten the hand on the flop, the first three cards. The Financial Advisor and the Banker whooped and high-fived her as she smiled and raked in her fake chips. "I didn't even know what I was doing," she beamed.

"That's my point," said the Guru. "You didn't have certainty or knowledge about the game, so you opened yourself to the knowledge that presented itself in the moment, whatever felt right to you. If you'd been an experienced player, you might have come out betting big and made me fold or been intimidated by my calling and folded yourself. Instead, you won a big pot. Getting past what you think you know and being humble enough to open your mind to whatever is in the moment is a powerful thing, but it's very hard to do. You have to be humble and brave enough to stop valuing what you know so highly."

"Wait," said the Banker. "What I know is valuable. What all of us know is valuable."

The Guru shook his head. "You're saying that your knowledge and the financial products are why your clients hire you," he said. "That's false, as we've learned. You are the value. Not what you know but who you are. Do you honestly think there aren't ten thousand other bankers out there who know as much or more than you do about accounts receivable financing?" He turned to the Stockbroker. "Do you honestly believe there aren't ten thousand other Series 7 license holders out there who know as much as you do about PE ratios?" He fired his gaze at the Financial Advisor. "And you, do you think there isn't a stadium full of reps who know more about dollar-cost averaging than you do?"

No one replied; the message was clear. "No," he continued, "your primary value isn't in what you know. It's in who you are. Who you are can become who you are destined to be—when you stop being so damned proud of what you know and start loving what you don't."

He flipped the deck of cards onto the table, where it stood edge-on for a moment before the cards tumbled into a pile. "Have any of you ever played Canasta?" he said. They all shook their heads, still reeling a little from his attack on their carefully acquired financial expertise. "Come on, now, don't be shell-shocked. I admire you all, seriously. You're passionate and smart and brave. You're just ready to face the harshest truth that what you pride yourself on so much isn't something to be proud of. Now, Canasta. No takers?"

Silence.

"How about Whist? Bridge? No? Why not?" He addressed the Banker.

The young man shrugged. "I don't know. Never had any interest in it, I guess. Never had anyone to teach me."

"Aha!" The Guru's shout made them jump, then laugh. "Sorry. You never had a teacher, and when we don't have a teacher to show us how to do something, what happens?"

The Financial Advisor said, "We make a lot of mistakes." He cocked his head, a gleam coming into his eye. "I think I'm starting to think like you. We don't like making mistakes, so we don't pursue new areas of knowledge because being new means we're bad at them. We stick with what's comfortable, what validates us."

"Beautiful!" crowed the Guru. "We are actually biologically wired to avoid areas of knowledge and experience where we're likely to make idiots of ourselves. We've talked about the amygdala, the center of our fear and rage. Now I want to introduce you to the anterior cingulate cortex or ACC."

"Hello," said the Banker dryly. The Stockbroker elbowed him.

"The ACC," continued the Guru, "is highly sensitive to dopamine, the neurochemical that gives us pleasure. Well, the brain is very good at recognizing patterns. Pattern recognition is a hallmark of humanity. When we encounter a stimulus, the brain predicts what will happen based on our past experience. If it's right, we get a shot of dopamine and feel good about ourselves. If we don't get it right, the dopamine cells flip us the bird, and we get nothing. That's a big negative shock to the brain. We want that dopamine; we're junkies."

The three students were sitting up straight and staring at him as he spoke.

"The ACC is involved in detecting errors in perception and prediction," he continued. "Whenever our brain makes a wrong prediction, the ACC generates a negative signal that's so powerful that many neuroscientists call this part of the brain the *oh shit* circuit. No dopamine for you! We want that dopamine, and what's the surest way to get it? Stick with the predictable, with what we know. Do what we're *good* enough at, guaranteeing we'll never get to *great*. We don't want to take chances, because we don't want the suffering that comes from not getting our dopamine fix. We want to feel good about what we do and know—but we don't realize that it's when we make errors that we evolve. We're not collections of neurons. We can learn and change our brains. That's called neuroplasticity. If we learn to view risky new areas of knowledge and errors as desirable, because they teach us and make us grow, we're not limited by our brains—we're empowered by them!"

"Wow," the Stockbroker said.

"Yeah," said the Guru. "The more you step into areas where you're ignorant, whether it's learning to juggle, speaking in public or quitting your job and starting a new career, the more you rewire your brain and connect the right and left hemispheres, intuitive and analytical. Basically, you become humble enough not to care whether you look like an idiot trying something you know nothing about, and you become smarter and wiser because of it."

The Accountability Factor

The Stockbroker stroked her chin and then lifted her head. "So not having an ego gives me a better chance of being a great poker player?"

"No," replied the Guru, shuffling the cards once more and tucking them into an inner pocket with the speed and dexterity of a master illusionist. "You still need an ego, but being great means knowing when to set your ego aside and be humble—to take pride in saying, 'I don't know. Teach me.' How many CEOs or financial wizards can do that?"

"Zero," said the Banker.

"Is that what you think I do?" asked the Stockbroker. "Cloak myself in what I know as armor against people who might judge me because I'm a woman?" She glanced around at all of them.

"We did," said the Financial Advisor.

She shot him a stern look, and he raised both hands in truce. "Hey, it's true. You came in here with a big chip on your shoulder, but it's gone now. I think it's because you realize that we don't care about what you know. We only care about who you are." He paused in thought for a moment. "I probably wouldn't have cared about that when this day—if it's still the same day—started, but it matters now. We're changing."

"Be a big damned waste of time if you weren't," the Guru said. The Stockbroker reached out and clasped the Financial Advisor's shoulder in thanks.

"So how do you become humble?" asked the Banker. "Eat humble pie?"

"Ooh, great band," said the Guru, closing his eyes and swaying to an unheard beat. "Never mind. How do you think you become humble, Funny Guy?"

"Me?'

"Yeah. You're close to graduation. You're smart enough to puzzle it out. Let's see what's under those sun-streaked locks of yours."

The Banker dropped his chin into his hands, closed his eyes and sank into thought. The Financial Planner got up and set some more wood on the fire. Outside, they could all hear spattering on the roof; it had begun to rain. After a minute, the Banker lifted his head and opened his eyes.

"You admit what you don't know," he started, looking hopefully at the Guru.

A scowl came back at him. "You can do better than that."

The young man frowned. "Okay. Next level down: you admit that other people know more than you do?"

"Getting warmer."

The Banker shrugged. "I got nothing beyond that," he said. "Help a brother out?" He looked at his colleagues. The Stockbroker said, "I think the next level beyond that is making yourself accountable, right?"

The Guru grinned. "That is exactly right," he said. "Well done, both of you. If you are humble, you are accountable for the consequences of your choices. Ulysses was accountable to his men, which is why he had himself strapped to the mast. He did not think that he was superior to them; what mattered wasn't his ego but his results. Most financial professionals are not accountable. How many of you have made yourselves accountable to anyone but your spouse or significant other?"

The three looked at the floor.

"So you're in a profession where you hold your clients accountable but you're not accountable yourselves?" he said. "If you want to start somewhere, start there. You can only lead people as far as you are willing to go yourself. Humility begins by making yourselves accountable to someone else, because you're saying, 'I have been my own worst enemy, knowledge is not enough, I place myself in your hands.'" He turned to the Financial Advisor. "Do you have a financial advisor of your own?"

"No."

"Why not?"

He gave a slantwise smile. "I guess because I know the markets," he said.

The Guru wagged a finger at him. "So why aren't you rich and retired?" he said. "Knowledge doesn't matter. Action matters. Investment maven Charlie Ellis once said in *Money* magazine, 'It's not the beginners who tend to die at skydiving.'[20] With knowledge comes arrogance and carelessness. No one is capable of being totally objective about their own affairs, no matter how much knowledge they have. Hemingway didn't edit his own books. Emotion takes over and that puts the amygdala in the driver's seat. Remember, you can't believe everything you think. If you're truly humble, you have to put yourself in the hands of someone else. Can you do that?"

"Me?" said the Financial Advisor. "Sure, I guess I could hire somebody to manage my portfolio."

"I'm not just talking about that," said the Guru. "I'm talking about being accountable in all things. Part of creating inevitabilities is making yourself accountable to other people in all the areas where you want change. Commitment without accountability leads to a lack of discipline. In what other ways could all of you make yourselves accountable to someone else?"

The Banker raised his hand. "If I want to get really fit, I would make an appointment with a personal trainer for tomorrow."

"Good one. What else?"

"I would sign up with Weight Watchers® to help me lose 20 pounds," said the Financial Planner."

"Right. What else?"

The Stockbroker said, "I would hire a life coach to help me get the hell out of this business before it suffocates me." They all looked at her, staring at her hands in her lap. She lifted her head and said softly, "I don't like what I do. I want something else out of my life."

They looked at her for a long moment. The Financial Advisor got up, walked over to her, crouched by her chair, and wrapped one long arm around her shoulders in a tight hug as she leaned into him. The Banker came over and wrapped both arms around them both. The moment raveled out for long seconds as the fire popped.

"Sorry about that," the Stockbroker said, sitting up and wiping her eyes. "I guess I didn't realize that until just now."

"No need to apologize," the Financial Advisor said. "I think we all feel that way at times."

She looked at him squarely. "Do you ever feel like you want out?"

He shook his head. "No, I love this business. I love that I can help people create a future. I don't like the way I've been doing it, but I wouldn't do anything else."

"It's your baby," said the Banker.

"What?" The Financial Advisor looked surprised.

"Men build businesses and buildings because we can't have babies," said the Banker. "I'm serious. We can't create life, so we create empires, explore the world, and invent things to compensate for that. I love what I do, too. I just want to do it on my own terms, not someone else's."

The Financial Advisor was looking for words when the Stockbroker chimed in. "Buildings and businesses are important. Where would babies live and how would we make money to support them otherwise?" She smiled at the two men. "It's all important. We all are." There was a long silence as they all regarded each other.

"Do you realize," said the Guru gently, "that's the longest time I've gone without talking since we started this?"

They laughed. "Yeah, you do talk too much, man," said the Banker.

"That was smart, all of you," the Guru said. "You're finally getting it. You admit you don't know where to go from here. That's humility. It's also empathy, something more people in your profession need. I suggest that all of you go out tomorrow and find your own financial advisor, stockbroker, or banker. Make yourself accountable to that person so you can fully understand what it's like. Begin changing your story."

What's Your Story?

"Our story?" said the Banker.

The Guru got up and started walking around the bar, turning off lights, closing cabinets, and shutting doors. As he moved, he said, "I said before that you were on a heroic quest. The hero journeys from ignorance and innocence to wisdom and accountability, and along the way, he or she confronts the darkest inner demons. That's mythic narrative, and we all have it. We're all living a heroic journey, but we've become so obsessed with the stories of reality TV stars that we've forgotten our own stories. We're told that if we're not famous, we don't matter, but we do. It's time for you three to begin rewriting your stories."

"How do we do that?" asked the Financial Advisor.

The Guru was washing dishes; the clinking sound was comforting in the quiet bar. "Well, first you take all the things that you think make you who you are, and you throw them over the side of the boat. What if you didn't earn money for a year? What if no one knew your name? What if you didn't have the suit and the car? What if you were stripped of everything you're attached to? Would you cease to exist? Of course not, but who would you be? What would you call yourself if you didn't know your name?"

The Stockbroker's eyes were shining. "Tearing up the current pages and starting fresh, that's what you mean," she said.

"Yes, but still remembering your past and letting it shape who you become," the Guru said, drying glasses with a towel. "This is about rewriting who you are, not just what you have done. How would you define yourself if you had no baggage from the past to drag behind you? Humility means becoming like a child. Until about age seven, children don't develop a self-contained sense of the past or future. They exist in the present unless we prompt them. That's why children don't worry, regret, or self-delude. What is, is. They are who they are. Imagine if you wrote your story like that but with the wisdom and experience of a 30-, 40- or 50-year-old?"

The Banker stood up. "That's Buddhist, man. I studied it when I lived on the West Coast," he said. "You're talking about getting rid of attachments."

The Guru nodded as he placed glasses back on shelves. "Yes, but most belief systems speak of letting go of attachments, as in 'Thou shalt worship no graven images.' For most of us, our identity is tied up in our attachment to things. How about this—when Gandhi was assassinated in 1948, his possessions were a beggar's bowl, a pair of reading glasses, and a loincloth that he made himself. That was his total material worth, but no one would have argued that was his total worth! He needed nothing to define himself. He was who he was. You are who you are, or you are who you become. If you can become humble enough to let go of what you know and what you have and become poor and ignorant, the whole universe opens up before you!"

He stopped and looked at them. "When you can let go of all things outside of yourself that you let define you, you're free to write your heroic tale in any way that you want," he said. "What is worth more than that?"

The Financial Advisor stood up and put on his suit jacket. It was clear to him that closing time was approaching. "You're not saying that we should give up our material possessions, are you?" he said. "I have three kids. It would be difficult to tell them they have to live in a hand-built log cabin in the woods."

"Of course not," said the Guru, wiping down the bar. "Material possessions and money aren't the problem. *Veneration* of them is. You can have a mansion and 10 Bentleys for all I care as long as you don't tie your identity to what you own, where you live, or what you do. There is a difference between the guy who drives the Lexus and the Lexus driver. Scratch the Lexus of the first guy, and he gets it fixed. Scratch the Lexus of the Lexus driver and you scratch *him*. He's defined himself by what he has and what he does."

The Banker coughed loudly.

"What's this?" said the Guru.

The young man looked at the floor with a grin. "I'm a Prius driver," he said.

They all laughed.

"You all have an incredible opportunity," the Guru said. "You have the opportunity to redefine yourselves completely, right here, right now. You can define yourselves by all the measures that matter: what you care about, what you believe, what your passion is, what you're willing to suffer for. Hell, you can even define yourself by your weaknesses, because they're part of you, and you should love them. The trick is that it's your story. It can go any way you want it to."

They thought about that for a moment. Unbidden, the Banker started straightening tables and chairs. The Financial Advisor went to the fire and poked the smoldering log with his foot, letting the fire burn out. The Stockbroker had a sparkle in her eyes. She slipped her arms into her jacket and said, "Everybody can do this, not just us, can't they?"

The Guru turned, walked over to her, and took her hands. "Yes, dear," he said softly. "That's what I'm counting on all of you to tell them. You can have regret about where you are or recognize it as an opportunity. I hope you can help them see that they should be exhilarated by the opportunity to face their brutal truth, find their purpose, discover their passion, and take action toward their epiphany. It's a matter of vision—you have to open your eyes. Look away from yesterday's errors and tomorrow's benchmarks and just be in the bloody moment for a change!"

Compassion and the Light at the End

They were all tidying up, making ready to leave, and feeling a bit wistful. The Stockbroker said, "I don't want to leave here."

The Banker walked over and put his hands on her shoulder and the Guru's arm. "The leaves are changing. Fall is coming. It's a great time to be alive, and I don't want to spend it in a stinky pub," he said.

"Didn't Mark Twain or the Dalai Lama say that?" said the Financial Advisor, walking over as well. The four of them stood together in the center of the darkened room. "I think I know what your final lesson is."

"What?" said the Guru. He headed for the green EXIT sign and opened the door to the outside. A crisp wind, redolent of autumn smoke and pulverized concrete from construction sites, rolled over them. The Guru locked the bar door, and they emerged into an alleyway different from what they remembered: narrow and dark, lined with tall buildings. The Guru waved them forward and trudged off. "This way. Enlighten me as we walk."

"Compassion," said the Financial Advisor. "Acceptance of what we have done and who we are, including all the mistakes we've made in their totality, because that's who we are. That's the path we had no choice but to walk. We need to love who we are and what we can become." He looked at them, and the Stockbroker took his arm. The Banker reached over and took her arm, reminiscent of the Dorothy-in-Oz posture they had adopted before. Perhaps they were not in Kansas anymore.

"Winston Churchill said this. Every day you may make progress. Every step may be fruitful. Yet there will stretch out before you an ever-lengthening, ever-ascending, ever-improving path. You know you will never get to the end of the journey. But this, so far from discouraging, only adds to the joy and glory of the climb," said the Guru. He was clearly leading them to a slowly growing point of light at the end of the long alleyway.

"What paralyzes people with regret is the revelation that they have always had the choice to rewrite their story but never did so," he said, his voice echoing. "We humans make mistakes, but this kind of thinking is not something we grow up with. It's something we grow into. As we said before, there are no rules. There's only humility before what you don't know and the most beautiful truth in the world."

"What's that?" said the Financial Planner. He, the Banker, and the Stockbroker stopped dead, watching their teacher. The Guru paused, walked back to them, and spread his hands wide.

He said, "If you don't know, you get to LEARN!" He took off at a hard pace, and they practically had to run to keep up.

"So what will you do?" the Banker asked the Stockbroker.

She thought and then smiled. "I will be for a while," she said. "Then I think I might go back to school. I always wanted to be a lawyer but never thought I could pass the bar. But I love the law. It's my . . ."

"Passion?" said the Financial Advisor.

"Yes."

"I'm going to go back to my office and fire some customers," the Financial Advisor said. "I'm going to throw out all my ties and start working from home a few days a week. I'm going to live the change, not lecture people. I'll be so happy and fulfilled that they'll beg me for my secrets." They were nearing the light now, seeing the glow of day on each other's faces. "What about you, cowboy?" he said to the Banker.

The younger man smiled. "I'm going to head for this incredible Italian place in Chelsea and have a fantastic dinner. Will you guys join me?" They hesitated, but he said, "Hey, we can't set out on our heroic journeys on an empty stomach, can we?"

The Stockbroker cocked one eyebrow at him. "All right. I'm going to figure out how I can bring my passion—nature, the oceans, and the environment—into my work. No, that's not right. I'm going to build my work around them. I finally understand that it's possible. That's what I finally realized."

"Do we do this together?" said the Stockbroker. They could hear the reassuring sounds of traffic now. The Guru was backlit by grayish Manhattan daylight.

The Financial Advisor turned to them as they walked. "I think we have to," he said. "Individually, each of us is an outlier, but together, we're enough."

"Enough for what?" said the Banker.

"To start a movement, maybe," the Financial Advisor said. His eyes shone with excitement and possibility. Together, they walked toward the street. The Guru had stopped at the edge of the alley, just shy of where the stained asphalt gave way to concrete sidewalk. Without a word, he smiled at them and hugged each of them in turn.

"Thank you," the Stockbroker said softly, kissing him on the cheek. "What exactly happened today?"

The Guru smiled again, then held out his arm and invited them to walk onto the sidewalk. As they did, the sun broke through gathering clouds to bathe them in brief gold.

When they turned, he was gone. The alley, in fact, was no longer a narrow, 19th-century corridor but a modern New York serviceway. A garbage truck sat there, waiting.

"And is anyone surprised by that?" said the Banker.

They all looked around. The sidewalks of the Financial District were crowded with people. Cabs and limos passed and the subsonic rumble of subway trains could be felt rather than heard under their feet.

"I feel like I just woke up," the Stockbroker said.

"Yes, I think that's right," said the Financial Advisor. He held out his arm again, and she took it. "Italian, huh?" he said to the Banker.

"The best."

"We need carbs. We have a lot of thinking to do. Shall we?"

They turned north and walked toward the corner together, looking around like tourists, to where they could hail a taxi.

Afterword

It doesn't take a great leap of insight to figure out that this book is about my own experience. No, I didn't actually navigate a deserted Manhattan and spend hours in a bar with a mysterious cosmic teacher, though I wish I had, but many of the stories told by "the Guru" are my stories. I've been attached to my financial accomplishments and devastated when my pursuit of a speaking career knocked me out of the top-five sales ranking I'd come to think was my birthright. I've put my family through rough times with my obsession with meeting benchmarks set by someone else. I've experienced the exhilaration that comes with realizing I was free to write my personal story in any way I wanted going forward. The idea of the blank page is absolutely thrilling to me. After reading this book, I hope it's becoming thrilling to you, too.

It may take multiple readings for you to absorb all the information here. I could have put much more in, such as more recent findings on psychology and the brain and self-transformation techniques from other leading coaches and teachers. The book could have been twice as long, but that would be self-defeating. My goal was to create something that was easy to read but impossible to forget. The important thing is not that I impress you with my insights but that you have your eyes opened to the truth. As my mother once said, "There is a lot of new information but no new truth." The truth is that many people in the financial professions are suffering.

It has nothing to do with up or down markets. It has to do with all the misguided thinking that the Guru describes: becoming focused on making your numbers, setting self-imposed rules and being bound by them, forgetting about what makes you passionate, and most of all, believing that your worth is based on how much you earn, what your ranking is, what your title is, and what you own. It's about, as Voltaire said, "Not letting perfect get in the way of good."

These are huge ideas, and they may be overwhelming when you're just trying to survive from day to day. I know—I've been there—but let me say this: if you don't start, you'll never change anything. There's one magic bullet that works wonders when you're trying simultaneously to redirect your life and career while trying to make a living:

GET HELP.

Together, We're Better

This book has been a humbling experience for me in many ways, but one of the most humbling has been the admission that I couldn't do it on my own. I've been talking about writing a book for years. After my speeches, one audience member after another has asked, "Steve, when's your book coming out?" My rote response was always, "Soon." In reality, I had no idea when it would happen. I kept deluding myself, just like the people in this fable, that one day I would somehow find the time to write the book, even though I had never written a book before. I fell victim to the lie that one day, things would somehow change. As the Guru says, things don't change. We make them change through our choices.

I asked around and was referred to Tim Vandehey, my coauthor. Tim's written more than 30 books; he's also a husband and father of two young kids, and a spiritual seeker like me, so I knew he would be a great fit. He was. He brought the clarity and no-nonsense drive that my project needed, and most importantly, he was able to get the manuscript written and capture my ideas with incredible clarity and vision. I learned a lesson in bringing this book to fruition: together, we're better. When we reach out, we grow.

I want to give you some advice for beginning to transform your financial practice, but I'm not going to talk about what you might expect. I'm not going to pimp software, new management techniques, or financial products. Remember, the value isn't in the products on the shelf; it's in the person sitting in your chair. I'm going to offer some ideas for changing yourself. Once you can start doing that, everything else falls into place, and it becomes impossible for you to do business the old way. My first piece of advice is this:

Get a life coach.

I have a life coach, and it's been one of the best decisions I ever made for both my career and my life. Life coaches are allies who are skilled at helping you break through the complexities of managing your current practice while doing the intense introspective work that's needed to discover where you want your life to go tomorrow. You can talk with a good life coach about managing your practice, managing your clients, making better use of your time, setting and reaching goals, putting accountability measures in place help you "create inevitabilities," and more.

It's important to be careful about hiring a life coach. Look for people who have completed accreditation programs certified by the International Coach Federation (ICF). That's a sign that your coaching candidate is trained and experienced. I suggest going to Lifecoach.com and doing a search. Connect with some coaches who have experience dealing with people in the financial professions. Do multiple interviews. Ask lots of questions. Most importantly, get references and take them seriously. No one who doesn't get sparkling reviews should be your life coach. This is your life we're talking about, after all!

Your Unique Ability

My second suggestion is this:

Outsource everything that you're not great at.

Dan Sullivan, the great executive coach, talks about your "unique ability." It's the one thing that you're best at and that you do like no one else can. Odds are that's what truly creates the value in your financial practice, whether it's client service, communication, empathy, asset management strategy, or one of a hundred other talents. Your life coach can help you isolate your unique ability, and when you figure out what it is, outsource everything else involved in your practice. Hire someone to open your mail, fill out paperwork, return calls, and so on. Why spend your time doing anything but the thing that creates the greatest value for your clients?

I suggest going a step further: fire clients who aren't your perfect clients. Why would you want to work with people who you don't enjoy and who don't appreciate your values? If the idea is simply too frightening, think about it differently. Divide your clients into three groups: A, B and C:

- A clients have been with you for a while, who "get" your values and character, and who appreciate that you're trying to give them what they need, not enable their bad decisions. You get about 65 percent of your income from them.

- B clients are less tolerant of your passion and purpose and more interested in asset allocation and products, but they're okay, because some of them actually understand that you're trying to empower them. You get about 25 percent of your income from them.

- C clients are customers. They take up more of your time with complaints and don't care about you. They just want product and investments. They have no loyalty. You get about 10 percent of your income from them.

Fire your C clients. As frightening as that may seem, why would you keep them? They don't bring in much income, and they waste your time. You don't like working with them. Refer them out to others. Stick with your A and B clients, and eventually plan to pare your list to just A clients. Over time, you will build a practice around people who share your values, care about you as you care about them, trust you to help them make sound long-term financial decisions, and help you earn a great per-hour income doing work you really enjoy. Imagine that! You'll spend more time doing what you do well with people who truly appreciate it and reward you for it.

Change Your Mind

My third piece of advice is this:

Don't believe everything you think.

Remember what I said early on about the need to think differently than your clients if you are to be a shepherd, not a sheep? That doesn't happen by wishing it. Your actions and words come from your thoughts, and to a great extent your thoughts and opinions are driven by what you read, hear, and watch. If you want to stop thinking like your clients and start thinking like the highly knowledgeable financial professional that you are, you need to be reading, listening to, and watching different sources of information!

Just say no to mainstream media. The news business is largely fear-driven, because the people behind it know that we're fear-driven. They can count on the amygdala to turn a terrorism threat, swine flu report, or stock market dive into a fear-driven ratings bonanza. Watch TV news some time and see how many stories are driven by the suggested fear of something that *might* happen: crime, bad weather, disease, war, household accidents, child predators, and so on. How often do these fears actually come to pass? Rarely, if ever, but we watch because it's hard not to.

Don't consume any finance- or economy-related television or radio that the average layperson consumes. Stay away from the over-simplified, irrational thinking that characterizes that media. Inoculate yourself from sheep-like thinking. Instead, watch and listen to any media, conservative and progressive, that expose you to smart people and sophisticated ideas. Discover the wonders of Internet radio, where you can find programs about finance, art, science, religion, and just about everything else.

The one thing you must do is *read*. Read everything you can get your hands on. Harry Truman said, "There are a lot of readers who are not leaders, but every leader is a reader." Read multiple books, but don't worry about finishing. Who said that you had to finish every book you start? If that were some ironclad rule, you'd only read small books! You are a leader; your clients count on you to know not only financial products but market trends, cultural influences, politics, and history. You need to become a Renaissance man or woman. Your book of business is dependent on your ability to lead, and your ability to lead depends on your willingness to read. Read magazines in your profession, both consumer and trade publications. Read things outside your profession, from technology to culture to history to science. If you're looking to learn what drives human economic choices, become a student of humanity in all its aspects. Read books on psychology, sociology, neurology, and anthropology, which will help you to understand why humans behave as we do. Buy five or ten books across the spectrum, and read the first chapter of all of them. If only four call to you right now, set the other six aside and pick them up later. *Read plenty of history*. Financial books are mostly about predictions, which are a fool's game. Read history, which is about patterns. If you know the behavior from the past, you can more adeptly predict the future.

If three or more people recommend a book to you, buy it and read it. You're being called to read it. If you think that sounds New Agey, fine, but trust me. It works.

Anne Sage says, "Read not to believe, but to weigh and consider." The only way to weigh and consider is to take the time to read and think. Don't speed read. Grant yourself the gift of "unrequired" time to read and ponder. Use the Internet. It's the greatest information and communication tool ever devised, and its filters can retrieve the information you want. Use services like Yahoo! News and Google News to create custom news feeds based on any subjects you like. Do it right, and you'll spend less time on what doesn't interest you and more time on what enriches you.

Make Yourself Accountable

My fourth and final recommendation is this:

Get a financial advisor.

If you don't have one already, hire your own financial advisor. It's about accountability. When I speak to groups, I'm appalled at how few advisors have made themselves accountable to anyone. You're in the accountability business!

Every financial advisor should have a financial advisor. You may have the information, but that's not enough. You need to manage your behavior and overcome your own human irrationality and bad habits, and to do that well, you need someone objective. You need your own financial advisor, because the primary value is not in the knowledge, which you have, but in the relationship. You should model the kind of advisor-client relationship you want by creating that kind of relationship with your advisor. Know and feel what it means to be a client.

Your goal is to become more fully a shepherd, not a sheep. To do that, you must have faith in the future. Faith and certainty are incompatible. The mind jumps to conclusions about the economy and the markets, because it hungers for certainty. If you rely on your knowledge alone, you will often jump to linear conclusions, deciding that whatever the markets are doing now will likely continue. What separates the shepherd from the sheep is faith in the future. Sheep are dumb animals that believe there's safety in numbers. History has shown, however, that in the financial professions, the herd is often led to the slaughter. Doing the right thing and sticking to your values and fundamentals can inoculate you against these human patterns of behavior. Your goal is not to become a great financial advisor; your goal is to become a great human being who happens to be an advisor. As the saying goes, when the student is ready, the teacher appears. When you become the person you are destined to be, the clients will follow.

A Four-Letter Word

The best investment you can make is an investment in yourself. Yet in the end, there's only one way you will consistently make this investment: *you have to go into it with love*. Love is not a word we usually associate with finance and investing, but that's not what we're talking about. We're talking about the evolution of a human being—you. Only when you value and love yourself and love who you can become will you take actions which, to be honest, can be lonely and scary at first.

As you walk the path I've described in this book, you may find yourself getting odd looks from colleagues. You might encounter angry or confused superiors. Your spouse might wonder if you've lost your mind. You might wonder the same thing. Take all those things as signs that you're on the right path. When you defy conventional wisdom, you'll run headlong into resentment, fear, and confusion. When you love what you're doing and trust the process, you'll gain priceless perspective and make yourself more valuable to those you serve.

We're all on a journey. This book is part of mine. Thank you from the bottom of my heart for sharing it with me.

Peace.

Appendix

LUCKENBACH LEAPS

Part of my goal with this book has been to share with you some of the truly profound thoughts of others, great thinkers who have influenced me. I call these timeless ideas "Luckenbach Leaps," because they inspired me to leaps in understanding—as I hope they will inspire you. I have captured them here for you.

> *Wisdom is knowing what to do next, skill is knowing how to do it, and virtue is doing it.*
> —David Starr Jordan, educator and writer

> *When you have the why before you, you can handle almost any how.*
> — Neitszche

> *The purpose of life is to live a life of purpose.*
> —Richard Leider

> *It takes great humility to see truth.*
> —Gandhi

> *Don't confuse motion with progress.*
> — David Gergen, professor of public service at Harvard's John F. Kennedy School of Government

The first reaction to truth is hatred.
—Tertullian

You can make money, or you can earn money.
—Lou Cassara

Never confuse prominence with significance.
—Rick Warren

Who you are being is far more important than what you are doing.
—Lou Cassara

Do not ask how to be a man of success, but set out to be a man of value.
—Albert Einstein

Success will follow you precisely because you have forgotten to think of it.
—Victor Frankl

The most difficult thing for people to understand about money is that money will come to you if you're doing the right thing.
—Michael Phillips

Growth means change and change involves risk, stepping from the known to the unknown.
—George Shinn

Courage is not the absence of fear, but the belief that there is something more important than fear.
—Ambrose Redmoon

To live is to war with trolls.
—Henrik Ibsen

Every day you may make progress. Every step may be fruitful. Yet there will stretch out before

you an ever-lengthening, ever-ascending, ever-improving path. You know you will never get to the end of the journey. But this, so far from discouraging, only adds to the joy and glory of the climb.
—Winston Churchill

LUCKENBACH LINES

I have also assembled a collection of what I feel are the best and most helpful ideas that originated from my own years of struggle and thought with the very issues I present in this book. I call these Luckenbach Lines.

- Spirituality often comes to those who have already been through Hell.
- Expectations = Market Correction[2]
- Losses hurt two and a quarter times more than gains satisfy.
- History repeats itself because behavior repeats itself.
- Strap yourself to the mast.
- The value in your practice comes from the character and purpose of the person in your chair.
- When you know *why* you do what you do, that will drive the how.
- An epiphany reveals the brutal facts we work hard to ignore.
- Knowledge alone does not lead to right action.
- You will not change things until you can face your brutal truth.
- The corrupting influence on most financial professionals is the undisciplined pursuit of more.
- The Inverse Square Law of Inspiration: the farther away a business moves from its starting point, the

less the founder's original passion and mission matter.

- You should be in business to serve, not sell.
- If you have customers, not clients, then you're nothing more than an order taker.
- You cannot serve people or your purpose when you are in fear.
- People are inspired by values.
- Money is not a reason to work, it is the result of work.
- Questions are the enemy of complacency.
- Force is giving people what they want instead of what they need.
- The angel's advocate fights a constant battle against self-interest that uses fear as its weapon.
- Faith is doing the right things and knowing that as a result, good things will always happen.
- You know what the right thing is, but you don't do it out of fear.
- Preparation frees you to act on faith and do the right thing in spite of yourself.
- We grasp at labels defined by other people to identify who and what we are.
- You must become what you want to achieve.
- Actualization, not motivation, leads to change.
- Actualization: Deep, irreversible self-knowledge that creates an irresistible need for transformation.
- When your need for change becomes stronger than the comfort in things remaining as they are, you will change.
- The value and meaning in taking action lies in taking the action, not in the result.
- Enlightenment has an expiration date.

- You must become in order to do, but then you must do in order to become.

- When you discover your needs and become the person who can fulfill them, you become what other people need.

- Change is hard. If it were easy, everyone would do it.

- The three great lies about change:
  1. Having the knowledge means you've already changed.
  2. You will make the changes sometime in the future.
  3. Some *sign* will tell you when it's right to step into that unknown future.

- You can't just decide to change; you have to feel that you have no choice.

- Your mission will feed your passion.

- Passion means suffering.

- Where you are is a product of who you have let yourself become.

- We shackle ourselves with self-imposed rules and rules we accept from others.

- Hack the epiphany.

- Fear will keep you where you are until you can find a belief that is more important than your fear.

- If you expect others to be accountable to you, make yourself accountable to someone else.

- Celebrate your weaknesses and the things you do not know.

- It's when we make errors that we evolve.

- Being great means knowing when to set ego aside and take pride in saying, "I don't know."

- With knowledge comes arrogance. Beginners don't die skydiving.

- Ask yourself who you would be if no one knew your name.
- When you free yourself from external definitions, you can rewrite your story.
- Love who you are and what you can become.
- If you don't know, then you get to learn.

LUCKENBACH LAWS

Some statements of this book are truths that I consider powerful, essential and timeless. They are my equivalent of irrevocable natural laws for the financial advisor. I have collected them here as Luckenbach Laws.

- *Sheep don't need other sheep. Sheep need a shepherd.*
- *The four most dangerous words in finance are "This time, it's different."*
- *The majority is always wrong.*
- *Preparation, not education or speculation, is the path to salvation.*
- *Knowledge is not sufficient to change behavior.*
- *Certainty is the enemy of change.*
- *The price of self-actualization is the death of comforting self-delusion.*
- *Your financial worth has nothing to do with your actual worth.*
- *Your values determine your value.*
- *Clients don't buy competence, they buy confidence.*
- *If you're powered by purpose, profit will take care of itself.*
- *You are worthy because of who you are, not what you do.*
- *Short-term right is almost always long-term wrong.*

- *Human beings only truly believe something after the fact.*

- *What you know doesn't matter unless what you do matters.*

- *Wanting things to be different is not the same as wanting to change.*

- *Love is stronger than fear.*

- *Knowledge without accountability is self-delusion.*

- *Humility begins with the admission that knowledge is not enough.*

Books to Read

- *A Whole New Mind: Why Right-Brainers Will Rule the Future* by Daniel H. Pink

- *As A Man Thinketh* by James Allen

- *Authentic Happiness: Using the New Positive Psychology to Realize Your Potential for Lasting Fulfillment* by Martin Seligman

- *Compensation and Self-Reliance* by Ralph Waldo Emerson

- *Endurance: Shackleton's Incredible Voyage* by Alfred Lansing

- *Everything Belongs: The Gift of Contemplative Prayer* by Richard Rohr

- *From Selling to Serving: The Essence of Client Creation* by Lou Cassara

- *Good to Great: Why Some Companies Make the Leap...and Others Don't* by Jim Collins

- *How We Decide* by Jonah Lehrer

- *LIFEonomics: Living Free of Worry and Regret* by Robert J. Holdford

- *Man's Search for Meaning* by Victor Frankl

- *Meditations* by Marcus Aurelius

- *Pathways to Bliss: Mythology and Personal Transformation* by Joseph Campbell

- *Retirementology* by Gregory Salsbury, Ph.D.

- *The Prodigal God: Recovering the Heart of the Christian Faith* by Timothy Keller

- *The Seven Habits of Highly Effective People* by Stephen Covey

- *The War of Art: Break Through the Blocks and Win Your Inner Creative Battles* by Steven Pressfield

Acknowledgments

This book has been a dream of mine, and there are many people without whom it would not have come to fruition. First, I must thank the two most important women in my life: my wife, for her love, patience and encouragement as I have strived to be the man she always knew I could be, and my mother for her love and faith. I must thank my colleagues at Jackson National Life for their enthusiastic support of my work and speaking, and Jackson management for allowing me to answer my calling. To Dr. Greg Salsbury, my friend and colleague, who introduced me to Behavioral Finance and put me on the road that led me to where I am today—for your encouragement and belief in me in the early days when I was often alone with my ideas, I am in your debt. A very special thanks goes out to my life coach and friend Dr. Curt Spear. He has guided me through some of my darkest days and helped me to see the errors in my thinking; I will be forever grateful. Finally, I have to thank my co-author and brother, Tim Vandehey, for capturing my vision perfectly and adding innumerable wonderful touches of his own.

About the Author

Steve Luckenbach is a Regional Vice President for Jackson National Life Insurance Company® in Ohio. With more than 24 years experience in the financial services industry, Steve is one of Jackson^{SM}'s highest producing wholesalers, and is consistently ranked one of the top Jackson wholesalers in the country. Prior to joining Jackson in 1995, he worked for SunAmerica and Bankers Trust.

Steve holds Series 6, 7 and 63 registrations, and is recognized as a "who's who" in the financial services industry. He is an engaging speaker known for his energetic presentations on behavioral finance, investor psychology, retirement, annuities and portfolio management. *Don't Believe Everything You Think* is his first book, based on those speeches. Steve lives in Cincinnati with his wife Rebecca and their children Gavin, Gabrielle and Grayson.

End Notes

1 P. Shinnick-Gallagher, *The Amygdala in Brain Function: Basic and Clinical Approaches* (New York: The New York Academy of Sciences, 2003).

2 *Housing Wealth Effects*, National Center for Real Estate Research, 2004. http://www.jchs.harvard.edu/publications/finance/w04-13.pdf/.

3 "Accidents, Fatalities, and Rates, 1989 through 2008," National Transportation Safety Board. http://www.ntsb.gov/aviation/stats.htm/.

4 *National Transportation Statistics* (quarterly report), U.S. Bureau of Transportation Statistics, 2009. http://www.bts.gov/publications/national_transportation_statistics/.

5 R. Hastie and R. M. Dawes, *Rational Choice in an Uncertain World: The Psychology of Judgment and Decision Making* (Thousand Oaks, CA: Sage Publications, 2001).

6 "Big rallies follow big stock drops, hint at bounces to come," Matt Krantz, USA TODAY, May 9, 2009

7 Stuart Wilde, *Silent Power* (Carlsbad, CA: Hay House, 1998).

8 "The U.S. Market for Self-Improvement Products and Services," Marketdata Enterprises Inc., September 1, 2006. http://www.marketdataenterprises.com/.../SIMkt2008PR-Oct14-2008.pdf./

9 A controversial first-century Christian Berber author.

10 At the 2009 Willow Creek Leadership Summit.

11 Lou Cassara, *From Selling to Serving* (New York: Kaplan Business, 2004).

12 "Economic Downturn Increases Rates of Homicide, Suicide," Kristina Fiore, MedPage Today, July 7, 2009. http://www.medpagetoday.com/Psychiatry/GeneralPsychiatry/14997/.

13 "Can you trust your financial adviser?", Liz Pulliam Weston, MSNMoney.com. http://articles.moneycentral.msn.com/RetirementandWills/CreateaPlan/CanYouTrustYourFinancialAdviser.aspx/.

14 David Roeder, "Primal Picks," *Chicago Sun-Times*, Jan. 14, 2007. http://www.suntimes.com/business/roeder/208997,CST-FIN-curious14.article/.

[15] *The Meditations of Marcus Aurelius Antonius.*

[16] Michael Phillips, *The Seven Laws of Money* (Boston: Shambhala Publications, 1996).

[17] "What If Your Business Was Truly All About Them?", Bill Bachrach, Financial Services Journal, 2004. http://www.bachrachblog.com/what-if-your-business-was-truly-all-about-them/.

[18] Paulo Coelho, *Warrior of the Light* (New York: Harper Perennial, 2004).

[19] Ambrose Redmoon, "No Peaceful Warriors!", *Gnosis: A Journal of the Western Inner Traditions*, Vol. 21, 1991, pg. 40-45.

[20] "Wall Street's Wisest Man," Jason Zweig; Charles Ellis, *Money*, June 2001. http://money.cnn.com/magazines/moneymag/moneymag_archive/2001/06/0 1/303368/index.htm.